TWO VIOLINS, VIOLINS, ONE VIOLA, A CELLO AND ME

Published in 2023 by Harcamlow Press Ltd
71–75 Shelton Street, London WC2H 9JQ
www.harcamlowpress.co.uk

ISBN 978-1-3999-3452-7

First published in German as
Muss es sein? – Leben im Quartett
in 2008 by Berenberg Verlag, Berlin
Second German edition 2021

Produced for Harcamlow Press by Otherwise
www. otherwise-publishing.co.uk
Design and typesetting: Simon Daley
Production: Angela Young
Printed in China

Sonia Simmenauer

TWO VIOLINS, ONE VIOLA, A CELLO AND ME

Translated by Gwen Owen Robinson
and Hartmut Kuhlmann

HARCAMLOW PRESS

CONTENTS

FOREWORD

by Arnold Steinhardt, first violinist
of the Guarneri String Quartet

Our Guarneri String Quartet first met Sonia Simmenauer while she was working for our then-European agent, the Hans Ulrich Schmid Concert Agency in Hanover, Germany. When Sonia left to form her own Impresariat Simmenauer, as she called it, the Guarneri Quartet went with her as one of the first string quartets on her new roster.

You might ask why we, an already well-known and successful quartet, would without question join her fledgling agency. The answer is quite simple. Sonia, despite her relatively young age, inspired utter confidence. She was (and is) smart, knowledgeable, personable, honest, and just so comfortable to work with. From the start of the Impresariat Simmenauer until the end of the Guarneri String Quartet's forty-five-year career, Sonia was our agent for Europe and beyond.

Granted, Sonia is a masterful concert manager. Year after year, she created exciting and rewarding concert tours for us all over the world. But there is one quality of Sonia's that especially endears her to me.

Sonia – perhaps because she grew up in a music-loving family – has a deep understanding of just how demanding a musician's life actually is. She knows that travelling with suitcase and instrument on planes, trains and taxis, a new hotel every day, food that might be exotic and wonderful or just as easily cause indigestion, all-consuming rehearsals, and finally the high-wire act of performing at top level night after night takes a mighty toll on a musician. Where another agent might prioritise that seventh concert in a row, that one more concert fee, Sonia would never forget the importance of a free day, and would encourage us to go to a museum, or to the movies to refresh our minds and bodies.

You, the reader, are in for a splendid adventure as you open the pages of Sonia Simmenauer's book. From her unique vantage point, she will take you into the inspired world of the string quartet repertoire and reveal the inner workings of concert management. You'll have a front-row seat, witnessing the life of some of the most distinguished string quartets of our era, and you'll hear the groups' artists speak with intimate understanding about music.

And finally, Sonia: deep thanks for our friendship, for our most fruitful professional life together, and congratulations on this remarkable and compelling book you have written.

Arnold Steinhardt founded the Guarneri String Quartet in 1964, along with John Dalley (second violin), Michael Tree (viola), and David Soyer (cello). Arnold is the author of two books, Indivisible by Four *(1999), and* Violin Dreams *(2006).*

FROM THE DAILY LIFE OF
A STRING QUARTET AGENT

———

BREMEN, APRIL

I have come from Hamburg for the concert, together with my assistant. On the pavement in front of the concert hall, we run into the violist of the quartet, he is pacing up and down with restless energy, smoking one cigarette after another. We greet each other cordially, then he explodes: he's afraid this is the last time he and I will see each other; he is going to leave the quartet after this concert, the rest of the tour is hereby cancelled. I nod, not commenting on this news, and ask how his family is. After a short while he excuses himself, he still has to practise. He takes the stage door, we take the main entrance. My assistant stares at me, aghast, didn't I understand what he just said, isn't that a catastrophe, how can I keep calm like that. After the beautiful concert, we go to a restaurant with all four musicians. It turns into a jolly evening. Late at night my assistant and I drive back home, and next morning, the complete quartet goes on to Düsseldorf for the next performance.

PARIS, FEBRUARY

Shortly after 5pm, a promoter calls in a panic. She fears for her concert. She has just listened to the rehearsal, the quartet was arguing constantly (she didn't understand a word, not knowing the language), until the

———

cellist left the stage in tears. What is she supposed to do now? I advise her to stay away from the rehearsal, to go and have a coffee and not to worry. I don't hear anything more. A few days later, I receive a letter enclosing a favourable review of the concert.

BAD KISSINGEN, JUNE

After a festival concert, a review comes out, saying, in brief, that despite their grim countenance, the four gentlemen had played marvellously. Too bad that audiences would never have this pleasure again, since it had emerged that the quartet would be disbanding after this tour. After a longish odyssey through every level of the newspaper, we get hold of the journalist and ask him where he got this – incorrect – news from. The journalist defends himself: it's common knowledge that the four members of the quartet are irreconcilably at odds with each other, that they don't want to have anything to do with each other outside the concert hall. But where could he have got this from? Some festival person had told him that he had received rather strict instructions for the hotel booking. The four rooms were to be as remote from each other as possible, neither directly next to each other, nor directly on top of each other. What would you expect him to think?

BONN, JANUARY

Shortly before a concert, three members of the quartet are sitting in the green room, plucking at their instruments and making jokes. The fourth is missing. I know that the fourth is supposed to travel separately and to stay in a different hotel. I ask, a bit nervously, whether they have heard from him, whether I should make enquiries – it's a quarter to eight, after all. They reply, slightly amused, that their colleague hasn't missed a single concert in more than thirty years. Abashed, but not really reassured, I leave the artists' room, take my seat in the audience and wait anxiously for the concert to start, preparing myself for catastrophe. At eight o'clock on the dot, the lights dim to indicate the beginning of the concert, the stage lights up, all four of them make their entrance.

BERLIN, NOVEMBER

I greet the quartet before their concert in the Berliner Philharmonie concert hall. We have arranged to meet afterwards in order to discuss further plans for the coming year. The musicians look strained, the atmosphere is leaden, but I don't dare ask what's wrong. The concert is odd, emotions seem close to the surface. Afterwards, I wait for them, they're still surrounded by enthusiastic listeners, old friends and former students. I feel it would be better for me to leave. I ask whether it's perhaps inconvenient to speak tonight, and offer to come back another time. They don't know yet, we would all have to go back to the hotel first, one of them has to call home. I still don't understand what's going on, only that it's serious. On arrival at the hotel, one disappears into the lift, the others sit down in the lobby, there's no conversation. Anxious waiting. When he reappears, they get up, look at him – and they fall into each other's arms, tears in their eyes. I feel so much in the way, everything is so intimate, I want to disappear. Soon they've recovered themselves, and explain to me that their colleague's wife had been expecting the results of a dreaded medical test today, and everything's fine. The evening winds up in a particularly cheerful way.

MUNICH, MAY

It's the end of a tour that had started out dramatically. Shortly before rehearsals began, it turned out that one of the members was seriously ill and had to undergo treatment immediately. It had been his fervent wish that the tour would not be cancelled, that he would be replaced by a former student. This evening, the cellist and I sit together after the concert and look back on this time that had been – emotionally and professionally – very challenging for all. The cellist tells me how he and his other two quartet colleagues had met after one of the first concerts for a beer in the hotel: exhausted, but happy having played a very successful concert against all the odds; sad and worried about their colleague who was ill, almost apologising for having played anyway, and confessing to each other: 'It's just that quartet playing is what we love to do.'

YOU WORK FOR MUSICIANS? HOW EXCITING!

———

By the eighteenth century, many famous artists were employing a secretary – someone who would take care of the administrative and practical aspects of the artist's life, and who would get paid by the artist for his services. Over the course of the nineteenth century, this secretary would develop into the impresario. The crucial difference was that the impresario – in many cases, if not always – would take on the economic risk of a concert, paying the artist a guaranteed lump sum and keeping the proceeds of the ticket sales for himself. (Sometimes, he would fail to pay the artist – there are entire books about spectacular scandals of this sort, with impresarios making fortunes and their artists being reduced to miserable poverty.)

Since that time, the work of the impresario has split into at least two different professions: the concert organiser or promoter, who sets up and advertises the actual concerts, and bears any financial risk involved; and the agent, who is on the side of the artists, keeping their diaries, and organising anything and everything related to their concerts, up to and including after-show dinners. Organisers and agents are two sides of the same concert-planning coin, and depend on each other.

I am an agent. Therefore, I formally work for the artists, representing their interests, but in practice, I am an intermediary between the artists and the concert promoters. The role is also about bringing the wishes of one party together with the ideas of the other, sometimes with diplomacy, and sometimes with cunning.

Artists' agents are both the most coveted and the most reviled people in the music industry. Coveted, because they are supposed to possess the key that opens the door to high-flying careers, and reviled, because they make a living from what their artists earn (percentages – commissions). They're accused of chivvying their artists around the world, regardless of the needs of art (or health) in order to get rich themselves. But to be honest, hardly anyone really knows what an agent actually does.

I began working at a concert agency in 1982. Many times, over the years, I've been asked about my job. When I answer 'I'm an artist's agent,' I am mostly met with an 'Ah' or an 'Oh', or even 'How exciting'. This is then followed by a host of questions:

'What does that mean: an artist's agent? Is that something like a broker?' – Yes, in a way, if only because we broker artists for a commission.

'Can I buy concert tickets from you?' – No, I don't deal with particular events. I don't belong to any institution that presents or sells concerts. It's more like I'm selling my artist to these institutions.

'Do you travel with your artists when they play their concerts?' – No. I do travel to some of the concerts, to see and hear my artists, but I don't travel with them.

'Do you pick the concert outfits? Do you go shopping with the artists?' – No way!

'You surely have a deep insight into the private lives of your artists. Are you good friends with them?' – No. As a matter of principle, I keep away as much as possible from the private lives of my artists. Of course, their private lives matter in the context of planning concerts and when it comes to questions of logistics. I can get a good feel for a lot of things from the trivialities of everyday business. Completely mundane questions can suddenly bring to light doubts, worries, frustrations, tiredness or utter weariness, fragility or insecurity. But if these private matters don't have any immediate repercussions for a concert, it may be that I never learn what they're really about.

And, no, I'm not good friends with my artists per se. A good, friendly relationship is welcome, obviously, which means a general mutual trust, respect, and the ability to talk to each other and laugh together. Some

QUARTETS REPRESENTED BY IMPRESARIAT SIMMENAUER SINCE ITS FORMATION IN 1989

Alban Berg Quartett	Novus String Quartet
Arditti Quartet	Pacifica Quartet
Artemis Quartett	Pavel Haas Quartet
Belcea Quartet	Petersen Quartett
Bennewitz Quartett	Prazak Quartett
Brahms Quartett	Shanghai Quartet
Brooklyn Rider	Škampa Quartett
Carmina Quartet	Tokyo String Quartet
Cleveland Quartet	Quatuor Ébène
Cuarteto Casals	Quatuor Modigliani
Guarneri Quartet	Quatuor Van Kuijk
Hagen Quartett	Quatuor Ysaÿe
Jerusalem Quartet	Schumann Quartett
Juilliard String Quartet	Simply Quartet
Keller Quartett	Vermeer Quartet
Kuss Quartett	Vogler Quartett
Leonkoro Quartett	

relationships are a bit more tempestuous; hardly any relationship is neutral. Being really good friends is not the basis of a professional relationship between agent and artist. Still, it is possible that a friendship – sometimes a beautiful one – grows out of it.

'Are you by any chance a musician yourself? Do you get involved in artistic matters?' – That's a very difficult question. I'm no musician, but obviously my musical ear has become more refined after all these years of hands-on 'training'. My role is not to judge whether an artist's interpretation is completely faithful to the score. It's more about determining whether an artist or a group – especially, of course, a string quartet – has a charisma that can reach out from the stage, or whether an artist is limiting himself by chasing after some kind of alien ideal. What I can do – and should do, sometimes – is ask questions, and, if possible, encourage an artist towards self-reflection, thereby setting a process in motion. How much of this can really happen inside the relationship between the agent and the artist remains very much down to the individuals. It should never be done heavy-handedly, and it should happen only on the artist's initiative. As an agent, you don't want to be perceived as delivering unsolicited bad news, in case you get shot as the messenger.

Actually, an agent's position is a fascinating one – hard to locate, and full of contradictions. You are right in there, with the artists at their most sensitive – working directly with them as they come to terms with their art, as they deal with the burden of their talent. This is exactly why it's especially important to keep the artists at a very warm arm's length – so, if they feel that you know too much, they are free at any time to treat you as an outsider.

A DEVOTED COMMUNITY

―――――

For someone who learns to play an instrument without the ambition of making it their profession, playing string quartets can become their ultimate goal. Those who master their instrument so thoroughly that they can tackle the scores of the great masterpieces of chamber music – and especially of string quartet music – face a wonderful future as amateur musicians. They possess a great treasure through which they will be able to share with others what cannot be replaced by any conversation, granting comfort against the frustrations and setbacks of everyday life.

Playing string quartets is not a profession in itself: the term 'string quartettist' doesn't exist! Playing string quartets is a certain way of playing music together and a commitment to a certain repertoire – anyone who has an affinity to this kind of music can devote themselves to it. A string quartet consists of two violins, one viola and a cello. The many string quartets meeting regularly in the private sphere to make music are the epitome of what's called *Hausmusik* in German. They have no 'name', nor do they perform in public, and they stay together as the same group, sometimes for decades.

However, these amateurs are not only eager instrumentalists; they also form the core of the chamber music audience. This is a knowledgeable audience that knows the text of the music, that criticises with merciless and well-founded precision. Nonetheless, this audience is also capable of great enthusiasm, because it knows and appreciates what is required for this collective performance, this declaration one is witnessing. Time and again, someone discreetly (or not quite discreetly enough) will whip out a pocket score and a sharpened pencil and busily take notes during a concert. In most cases, this is no critic, punctiliously sketching his review against the backdrop of the score; more likely it's an alert amateur musician, fortifying himself with arguments for his own next rehearsal. Now and then, a listener, score in hand, approaches the artists after the concert and wants to discuss, or even argue about some interpretation or other that 'sounded strange' to him. He won't always be welcomed enthusiastically!

Compared to audiences at orchestral concerts, big solo recitals or even operas, which all, more or less, resemble (or actually are) social events, the string quartet audience comes across as a small, devoted community of music lovers who attend a concert the same way lovers of literature attend a reading or a philosophical evening.

What a devout community! Whenever an organiser comes onstage at a string quartet concert to announce a change of programme or a change of dates, I always have the fantasy that they're about to deliver a sermon.

String quartet music seems not to be for young people. That's the impression you get when you try to calculate the average age of a quartet audience. If you end up with an average of fifty years, you happen to be in a concert attended by a surprisingly young audience. The age gap between the artists and the audience stands out, especially when young quartets are playing. The fact that you don't see too many young audience members may be to do with how string quartet concerts can come across: even if they aren't necessarily quiet, they can seem serious, introverted and long. The same four people onstage for more than two hours, without any change of set, without any motion to speak of, without grand effects like the deafening noise of a gigantic orchestra or the fascination of a small figure (standing) in front of a sea of musicians (sitting), a single voice rising above everything. No, it's just four people, sitting more or less in a circle, 'having a conversation'.

It's not so much the perceived quiet form, it's the reputation dogging the string quartet that deters young people. The string quartet has been – and still is – regarded as highbrow, rather more elitist than popular, which is why the listener who doesn't know too much about music expects it to be difficult to access and to understand. This may be the reason why most chamber music concerts are organised by private chamber music *Vereine*[1]. These traditional societies – which, from a modern point of view, you might call self-help groups – are set up by aficionados who just want to hear their kind of music actually performed.

From the *Gesellschaft der Musik- und Kunstfreunde Heidelberg* (Heidelberg Society of the Friends of Music and the Arts) website in 2004:[2]

The society ... was founded in November 1945, shortly after the end of the second World War. Hunger for good music and good art, especially for that which had been prohibited under the Nazis, made committed citizens resort to self-help. The society organised its first concerts and art tours under the most difficult circumstances (old chronicles report that concert-goers were asked to bring wood and charcoal so the concert hall could be heated a little). Members of the board and the advisory committee, as volunteers and in their spare time, take care of organising and running the concerts, from checking tickets and selling programmes to looking after the artists.

---

1 In Germany a *Verein* (plural: *Vereine*) is a registered club, association or society, typically with charitable goals.
2 This website has ceased to exist.

Audiences of this kind are dedicated to the cause. They intimidate non-experts, who can't join in discussions about the proper tempo, or the repeat that wasn't played in the third movement. And they put young people off – with their bourgeois ways, and because of their age. Hence, the concert promoter, the *Verein* itself, constitutes the audience.

I asked Harry Jahns, chairman of the *Verein Iburger Schlosskonzerte* (Society of Iburg Castle Concerts), if he would write something for me about his motivation.

Dear Frau Simmenauer,

I am a passionate amateur violinist and violist! Together with two friends, I have played in the same string quartet for a quarter of a century, without ever really making any progress. We have the occasional performance at exhibition openings in the local bank or at club anniversaries.

Two things prompted the founding of our chamber music series: the lovely Early Baroque Hall of Knights in the castle, and self-interest. As far as the latter is concerned, I have to tell you that, whenever I invite a string quartet, a piano trio or a piano quartet, the programme always has to include one work that we ourselves – with the requisite cast of musicians – can master, in our own preparation for the concert. This not only increases our own pleasure in listening, it also helps me to find appropriate introductory remarks about the forthcoming concert – something I certainly don't always manage! – or something I can write in the invitation letter I send out to our regular clientele.

My team is a godsend. We do almost everything by ourselves, from collecting adverts for the programmes and distributing posters, to running the box office and organising the wardrobe. For example, a former pharmacist handles all our tax and other financial issues. But! No one gets to tell me how to do the programming! The only principle in programming is that we're not particularly fond of 'crossover' (no arrangements, if possible), and that we offer intense, eventful chamber music. Most of our listeners come from nearby Osnabrück, and since the number of regulars has only gradually increased, it's only been for the last five years that we have managed almost always to have a full house.

I would be really delighted to hear from you, and send kind regards!

Harry Jahns

Associations like *Vereine* have their rituals and their histories, too, of which their members are proud. For decades, the same table in the same restaurant gets reserved for the 'dinner after' with the artists, or certain members 'take turns' hosting a late dinner. Any quartet that has ever performed in Hamburg can tell of the famous evenings put on by Herr Jung, the chairman, who held that office for decades, and his wife. These evenings would include the detailed contemplation of Herr Jung's own beautiful Amati cello. Afterwards, Herr Jung would sit next to the quartet's cellist, and the two would discuss vast portions of the string quartet repertoire, as fellow cellists do.

Herr Dr Sprengel, owner of the Hanover chocolate company and a great patron of the arts, was chairman of the *Kammermusikgemeinde* (Chamber Music Community) in Hanover. He navigated the universe of string quartets effortlessly, like a pianist playing with his eyes closed. He knew them all – many of them personally – and he knew exactly who had played which works in Hanover, when, and, most particularly, how. The articles of the Verein required an annual members' meeting, for reporting on the accounting year, and for filling the various board positions, such as deputies, treasurers, etc., by election or re-election. Dr Sprengel was not only the chairman. He was also, and to a high degree, patron of the association. He effectively led the Chamber Music Community all by himself, making the decisions about artists and programmes. He did abide by the *Vereinsregeln* (the rules) that called for an annual meeting, and did use the newspaper classified ads as they required – except that, every year, he would place them in a different section, where no one would have expected to find them (such as among the adverts for removal companies, or animal care). The quorum required for taking decisions would be invited personally, according to Dr Sprengel's private criteria.

It almost seems here as if it's the audience inviting the artists personally, in order to have those pieces they themselves struggle with in their own living rooms performed onstage. As a result, the artistic demands on the professional musicians are exacting. The story goes that one very experienced organiser banished a famous quartet from his programmes for years just because of an omitted repeat.

Nevertheless, the topic generates a deep community spirit, because everyone shares the same fate before the music, regardless of whether they are onstage or in the living room. Many an amateur quartet chooses its private repertoire by reference to the programmes of the local concert series, and regard the concerts as a kind of lecture or lesson. Others exercise their influence within the Verein to invite those artists who are able to play exactly the programmes they want to hear. Of course, the 'familial' character that contributes to the special atmosphere of chamber music concerts and inspires the comparison of philosophical evenings has a flipside, which I would call conservativism. The great joy, the basis of all the volunteer efforts, is more about nurturing and promoting the well-known, leaving only a little room for what's new and, on first hearing, alien.

The venerable and very conservative *Gesellschaft für Kammermusik Basel* (Basel Chamber Music Society) had noticed the young Alban Berg Quartett, and eventually invited it to play its debut in their concert series. The invitation included certain stipulations: in particular, the programme must not include modern pieces. A surprising thing, since at that time Basel's musical life had long been under the influence of the great patron and interpreter of new music, Paul Sacher. The programme the quartet had proposed included the 'Six Bagatelles' op. 9 by Anton Webern – these would, therefore, need to be replaced. This was no small dilemma: the Alban Berg Quartett made a point of never playing any programme without at least one work from the twentieth century. On the other hand, principles aren't worth too much if no one wants to pay attention to them. To get the platform from which they could point the way to new musical horizons, the quartet needed to attract an audience. So, they gave in and accepted the restriction. Webern did not appear on the programme. During the applause, just before the audience got up to leave for the interval, Günter Pichler, the quartet's first violinist, took his chance to address them. He announced that the quartet would now be playing the 'Six Bagatelles' by Webern, and that whoever did not want to listen would be free to leave the hall. Not a single listener left. The audience received the work with deep concentration – and, afterwards, erupted into thunderous applause.

WHY STRING QUARTETS,
OF ALL THINGS?

———

People presume all the time that I play string quartets myself: there couldn't possibly be any other reason for insisting on specialising in string quartets. So, I never fail to surprise when I confess that I don't play in a string quartet, that I have never even mastered a string instrument, and that I long ago shelved the piano playing.

I grew up in a suburb south of Paris. My father opened his paediatric surgery there, in a housing estate that was built in the sixties. The grown-ups said, 'This is Paris.' But for us children, the city seemed unattainably far away – and it was even worse for us as adolescents. At home, we spoke only French, and our parents told us we *were* French. Yet I always felt alien. Some things seemed mysterious to me. On certain days, when most of the girls in my year went to the newly built little church where they were prepared for their first Communion, I wasn't allowed to join them. I didn't understand why. My father would frequently have phone conversations in German. And time and again, people would come to our home, mostly musicians, and he spoke German with them, too. These people lived in America or Israel or even further away; they would be staying in Paris for a concert, for a conference, or simply on their annual trip to Europe, and they would come to visit us. On such evenings, music would be played, string quartets whenever possible,

———

and there would be a lot of conversation, during and after the music. Although I didn't understand the language, I sensed that completely different worlds came to life on those evenings. Once we got a little older, my father told us of the time before the war, of skating on the frozen canals of Hamburg, of weekends in Lauenburg, and of the Grindel Talmud and Torah school where he had to go after he wasn't allowed to attend 'normal' school any more. After his retirement, he agreed to write down his memories for us, about his childhood in Hamburg and the years of the war in France. The little book became particularly precious to me when my own children were old enough to read it themselves.

In my family, Hausmusik, *chamber music, had a long tradition. My grandfather, a renowned advocate, played string quartets every week with the leaders of the Hamburg Philharmonic.*[3] *Sadly, I never heard them, because in 1933, he emigrated to Antwerp: at that time, I was six years old.*

Moreover, he invented a clever ruse in order to take his fortune abroad with him (which was strictly forbidden in Nazi Germany). He bought an entire string quartet: four instruments by the brothers Hieronymus and Antonio Amati.[4] *These were easily taken across the border, because they weren't new! In the years after the war, in Paris, I had custody of this quartet until it was sold for the joint heirs.*

My father's family fled the Nazi regime in 1938, when my father was eleven years old, going from Germany to Paris. Like many assimilated

---

3 I learned recently that my great-grandfather was one of the active founders and patrons of the *Hamburger Philharmonische Gesellschaft* (Hamburg Philharmonic Society) a foundation that to this day supports the Hamburg Philharmonic Orchestra.
4 The instruments were cared for by a Brussels museum, where they were deposited in the basement along with the goods of many other fleeing Jewish families; they were kept there during the war, next door to an ammunition depot, as it later transpired. None of them came to any harm.

Jews, they had decided to emigrate very late. Shortly afterwards, when the Germans came marching in, they had to flee once more, further south. In the south of France, in hiding and using false identities, they only just managed to get through the war. Afterwards, they settled in Paris.

I'd already started learning to play the cello in Hamburg. During the war years, hiding in France, I spent my days practising the cello, because going out was dangerous. After the war, in Paris, someone approached me one day, pointing at my cello:

'Are you an amateur?'

'I am.'

'Then I've been looking for you.'

Thevernot was the violist of a POW quartet that had played through the classical repertoire in the camp. Pigot, an engineer, was first violinist, and his sister was a professional pianist on the radio. Bijou, as the violist was called, was training as a gynaecologist. The cellist had died, and so I was invited to step in for him. The first thing that was put on my plate was Mozart's D Major quartet.[5] What an impertinence!

The philosopher Theodor W. Adorno describes his image of an ideal musical education as that of a child lying in bed late in the evening and listening to his parents playing chamber music in the living room. 'In the time which has been stolen from sleep,' he wrote in 1957, 'this child will penetrate deeply into the secret cells of music, much more than if he had been dragooned for years into participating in organised playing groups.'

Ever since I can remember, I have heard string quartet music and the German language, so for me, they belong closely together. They

---

5 Mozart's string quartet no. 21 in D major, K 575, one of the so-called Prussian Quartets, is notorious for its great technical challenges especially for the cellist.

represent the lost world in exile, the language and colour of the past. I mastered neither of them, and yet the two of them have evolved as main components of my life. I made a profession of the string quartet, German became my main language, and it's the mother tongue of my children. Thus, the string quartet – and the German language, which, to my mind, belongs to it – is the bridge to the world of my father's family, to my origins in German Judaism, and eventually to Judaism itself.

As chance would have it, my first permanent position was as a *Kammermusik-Sachbearbeiterin* (chamber music 'clerk' – that was the job title!) with the concert agency Schmid in Hanover, and among the first artists given to my care were the Guarneri Quartet, the Alban Berg Quartett and the Cleveland Quartet. I was joining a very sophisticated organisation, where everything was precisely defined and neatly organised. But the individual peculiarities of artists can't be filed anywhere. So, my artists at that time had to train me on the job – with varying degrees of patience – until I, eventually, managed to win their confidence and be accepted as a partner.

The artists did not restrict themselves to issuing directives. They explained them to me, in detail and in full colour. They told me stories from their travels; they gave me descriptions of the halls in which they played, of their acoustics, size, and atmosphere, of the peculiarities of the promoters and of the audiences in different places and countries. They described the character of the works to me, and explained the way they assembled their programmes, pointing out that a programme isn't good if the listeners are sent back home in a gloomy, depressive mood, as would happen if, for example, Shostakovich's String Quartet no. 15 was combined with Bartók's String Quartet no. 6 in the same programme. They made it clear to me that manageable travel distances to and within a concert city, decent green rooms and the attendance at rehearsals of the lighting technician and the stage manager are all essential factors in the life of a travelling musician, and that a successful concert depends on them. A room next to the lift is a nocturnal scourge in any hotel, regardless of how modern and silent the lift might be. At many hotels we book for our artists, we try to find out which are the 'lift rooms', and we explicitly ask for them not to be given to our artists. My artists taught me all this and much more, each one in a slightly different way. I learned that their demands were not diva-like affectations but simple – sometimes desperate – attempts to create conditions that made it possible for them to carry out their profession with undisturbed concentration.

When I founded the Impresariat, my own agency, in 1989, I explicitly declared that I intended to run it exclusively for string quartets. Many derided my decision, considering me a lunatic and commercially suicidal. Only the string quartets – not just the ones that were my clients but many others as well, as I learned over the course of later years – were grateful to me, because they were given full and proper status. They were no longer an embellishment to a list: they were at its centre.

I couldn't have made (and survived, financially) the step to found my own business if it hadn't been for artists like the Alban Berg Quartett, the Guarneri Quartet, the Tokyo String Quartet and the Cleveland Quartet, who encouraged me and made their own decisions to follow me. After all, for them, it meant leaving a very well-established and respected agency to help a young agent establish her own reputation. The risk they took was manageable, because by that point, we knew each other well, and had done for a long time. They had all been my teachers, and they knew that I'd already built up my own relationships with many promoters. A few years later, the first soloists joined my list, looking for what they called 'chamber music treatment', which is hard to define, but was meant as an antithesis to the commercial rat-race of soloists.

ON TOUR

―――――

One day, Günter Pichler, first violinist of the Alban Berg Quartett, lost his patience. I had sent him a list of cities for one of their upcoming concert tours. Reading the maps, everything had looked reasonable and logical to me, although I hadn't checked the itineraries in detail. Three or four hundred kilometres didn't seem that far to me – it's just a few centimetres on the map. He asked Herr Schmid to allow me to go on tour with them for a few days – I think it was three days – so I would finally understand what it meant to travel. The part of the tour that I joined was, in principle, uncomplicated: everything was easily manageable by train (there was only one change on one of the routes). Altogether, travel time between hotels was never more than four hours. I returned home as exhausted as if I'd made the entire trip in a badly sprung stagecoach. And yet I had nothing to do but tag along, while the artists, on top of the travelling, had to practise, rehearse and play concerts. I had only a small suitcase for three days, the musicians were dragging large suitcases for a four-week tour, including concert clothes and music, as well as their instruments. On trips like that, the clock ticks particularly fast: packing in the morning, paying the hotel bill – it seems that all the other hotel guests want to pay at exactly the same time – stowing the luggage in the taxis in a reasonable way to avoid ordering a third taxi, finding the right platform at the station, the escalator is out of service, there's a crowd in front of the carriage location indicator, the carriage is at the far end of the platform. In the train, it's a tight fit, the luggage is bulky and has to be heaved up on to the racks. At the destination, there aren't enough taxis available, there's a queue, it's raining. In the next hotel, the instructions for the reservation – quiet rooms, far away from each other – have been ignored, and the lady in reception doesn't understand why this should be such a problem for just one night. Unpack, find some quiet minutes before getting ready for the evening. How far is the concert hall? Is it possible to walk, to get some fresh air, maybe to find a sandwich somewhere along the way? The janitor at the artists' entrance hands over the green room keys in exchange for a signature, muttering: 'Third floor, left-hand side, behind the glass door.' Where's the lift? Or are there only stairs? How do you get from the green room to the stage? Where is the promoter who knows his way around and can guide you? The chairs on the stage are useless: the legs are too short; the seats are upholstered in red velvet so they will get hot if sat upon for any length of time; they're old and probably not very solid. Someone imagined that it would look nice, like in a castle, back in the olden days! The lighting has to be set up so that the music is lit but the musicians don't get dazzled. Eventually, everything is sorted enough for the rehearsal to begin. One of the musicians walks down the aisles to check the sound: each hall is different. The firefighters come and want to check the safety curtain, that's the rule. Then the usual fight for the admission of the audience. The quartet wants to rehearse onstage for as long as possible, the hall managers want to open the hall for the audience as soon as possible. Are the tickets for the musicians' friends set aside at the box office? Coffee, water and tea are provided in the green room, but the cellist is unwell, he needs peppermint tea. Actually, he just needs hot water – he brought his own tea bag. Where's the canteen, or is it just a kitchenette?

Half an hour to go till the concert, checking clothes, everyone has their own way of concentrating, one thing or another is discussed briefly. The concert starts. It's only this moment that counts. It doesn't matter any more whether this was a travel day, where you have come from. After the concert, friends and strangers flock, the tension eases. But soon, time's pressing again, you're collecting stands and music, there's a reservation at a restaurant, but the kitchen closes at 11pm, everybody's hungry. Back at the hotel, it's well after midnight – and the train tomorrow morning leaves shortly after 9am.

All of this requires a great deal of training and routine – and discipline. Those few days on the road with the quartet became one of my most important lessons.

Living as a string quartet means a life of travelling. Sometimes it's just a few days, sometimes it's many weeks, all of which the members spend in close companionship. The quartets mostly travel in their group of four, particularly during big tours – because of the obviousness of doing everything together, for purely practical and economic reasons, out of an aversion for travelling alone, or simply out of habit. Travelling has many mundane aspects, and it's exactly these components that cause intimacy. It has to do with waiting, with waiting for each other (there's always one, always the same one, who's almost late – another one, always the same one, arrives well ahead of time), with waiting together (for a train, a flight, a taxi, before a concert, after a concert). It has to do with simultaneity: together and at the same time, they encounter new countries, new cities, new halls, new people. It has to do with 'being strangers together' and with recognising, every so often, that they are strangers to each other, too. They experience many things together, but they don't necessarily share what they have experienced. And then there are circumstances that force them to share moments with each other, even though those moments are exactly the kind of things you want to share only with a person who is very close to you. On a journey, on a tour, anything that happens to one of them individually concerns all four of them: an individual grief doesn't remain hidden, a bad night can't be concealed, a bad tooth is everyone's worry, a lost suitcase might hold the music for the next concert. When I had a phone conversation with the cellist of a quartet and asked after the recalcitrant finger of his colleague, he told me: 'What we have here is not one of his ten fingers, but one of our forty fingers. So, it's *our* finger.'

Donald Weilerstein, first violinist and founding member of the Cleveland Quartet, never forgot a single note, but otherwise forgot pretty much everything else. One morning, I receive a phone call from the manager of the hotel in Recklinghausen where the quartet had stayed for the night. The chamber maid has found the first violinist's tails in the wardrobe and his patent leather shoes sitting under the bed. The quartet is on the train already, on their way to the next concert in a small town in southern Germany. Even with the special courier that is organised straight away, it is too late, the tails can't be delivered before the concert. Finding a costume rental isn't going to work either because it is a religious holiday in southern Germany. Nowadays, almost no one performs in tails; at that time, in 1985, the dress code was still very conservative. The quartet, too, was very conformist in these matters, and so the tension between the four of them becomes enormous. No one can go onstage like that! The promoter is able to help, in her wardrobe, she has the tails of her recently deceased husband. She has to overcome her own feelings, but eventually finds comfort in lending them. They are far too large, not even braces can solve the problem. As for the shoes, it's all too late, he has to perform in his street shoes. The violinist rehearses standing up, while the lady sews him into the oversized trousers. No one can help laughing. The evening is saved.

You inevitably meet as early as breakfast, unmade-up, tired out, vulnerable. You know everyone's little noises, the peculiar ways everyone has of thinking, sleeping or playing, the different kinds of breathing, who blows their nose when, how, and how many times. You know all the little rituals everyone develops, and at which you can only laugh or scream, depending on your mood. The rehearsals, lasting for many hours, come with an inevitable lack of physical distance. You know the others' smells as well as if you all lived under the same roof, so that, after years, you either don't notice them any more, or you feel as if you can't bear them any longer. Playing an instrument brings out a person's hidden traits, things that aren't apparent in normal interaction: a physical posture, a wheeze, an absorption in certain moments.

Sometimes you take offence at quirks that have embarrassed you again and again: the way someone laboriously recalculates his restaurant bill, ponders the size of the tip he's intending to give, the way he always wants to explain a shorter, better route to the taxi driver, the way he feels compelled to tell bad jokes whenever there's a new audience, thereby making any sensible conversation impossible. Someone deals with people in an aggressive way while you would just like to be nice; you're standing there and can't do anything except try to compensate with a forced, awkward smile. So many everyday situations that have nothing to do with music.

Certain reactions, certain phrases, become predictable; you even learn to mimic them. When it comes to ordering in the restaurant after the concert, one member of the quartet is missing – he's outside, on the phone. Perfectly capturing his tone of voice, the other three chant in unison: 'One entrecôte, still a little pink, with lots of chips.' When the fourth returns to the table, he's told that they have ordered for him. He looks at the menu and says he really hopes that they ordered an entrecôte, still a little pink, with lots of chips. Rituals, gestures develop, a distinct language. You know the way the sentence someone's started will end, you already know when something is coming, and you prick up your ears only if it doesn't come. Individual words work like codes, containing entire stories no one else understands. Shared day-to-day life brings, again and again, situations in which a well-attuned group communicates ever more economically, oftentimes with just a glance, a gesture, barely perceptible to anyone around them.

Frictions and arguments are cultivated that aren't really frictions and arguments, and many an amiability can, in reality, be a nasty sideswipe. You know each other by heart; it becomes a matter of instinct. This, of course, involves the danger that you get so accustomed to each other that you don't really perceive each other any more. The paths of understanding are so well trodden that small changes don't get recognised. Familiarity is presumed, and becomes constricting. All these things by themselves could just mean that there's a team, but then there's the music, there are rehearsals and concerts.

INSIDE VIEW

––––––––

For a long time, I was cohabiting with the Brahms Quartett – almost literally. Dieter Göltl, the cellist of the quartet, was my first husband. My first little office was in our flat, next to the room that would become the quartet rehearsal room. Unavoidably, and sometimes reluctantly, I followed the four men struggling to piece together their four voices. At times, it was absolutely agonising. A few bars of music, followed by endless discussions. I couldn't hear the words in detail, but the music and what it conveyed cut very clearly through the wall. The same bars again and again, sometimes slower, sometimes faster. A sudden interruption – except that someone carries on playing a few bars by himself. The predictable, irritated request of someone else – could he please stop playing, there was something to discuss, wasn't there? If one doesn't understand the words that are spoken, if one just hears the tone and pitch of the voices, an odd music emerges, a different kind of string quartet playing. First, someone says something, then all four voices mix together, in layers; one voice gets louder, one speaks faster to prevent interruptions, short and snappy remarks flare up. It might happen that one drops out of the discussion altogether, his silence growing louder than the voices of the others. The same happens when someone stops in the middle of playing. It takes a while for a bystander, who isn't watching and doesn't really know the score, to realise that something is missing. It's just that something sounds different, some pressure is building. Whether in discussion or in playing, the latent – or open – aggression between these four men could transmit an almost unbearable tension. Time could wear on forever, even when I wasn't listening, or didn't want to listen. Eventually, they would either settle for today's preliminary results or push on with another passage. Pushing on, though, could mean either a breath of fresh air or a fresh conflict. There were other acoustic images, too, when they began to play and just played on, enjoying their playing, and I got an inkling of their unity and the natural unanimity of their breathing. Their joy, their relief in laughter, transferred itself to me. I could sense a gentle embarrassment creeping up on them as their eyes were opening to each other. It was as if they were newly in love.

I was able to live through a string quartet's everyday life in my own home. I gathered valuable glimpses of the internal life of a string quartet, even if no one string quartet is like any other. For a long time – which I might call here my apprenticeship – I focused on learning the ropes of my profession, on understanding the mechanisms at play between artists and promoters, and what troubles each side. I got a grip on disaster management by developing nerves of steel for the daily 'mishaps', and above all, by ending up with the consoling insight that, as long as it's not a question of life or death, there's almost always a solution.

What if, for example, the railways decide to go on a wildcat strike and not a single train is running, not even the one that was supposed to take the artists to their next concert venue? The car rental places are overcrowded. Who do you know in this unfamiliar city who would lend a car, one big enough for four people with their instruments – always that cello! – and their luggage?

Or what if the violist of the quartet has his bag – where he keeps his music – snatched from his hand in Milan railway station? The police are brought in immediately, they sympathetically record the incident but leave no hope of ever recovering the bag. What's on the programme? A local music shop has two of the works in stock, the owner agrees to photocopy the viola parts and deposit them at the hotel reception so that the violist can pencil in a few things from memory once he gets there. But the third work is not in stock. Who else might have the piece in their repertoire and happen to be at home, so you could call and ask them to photocopy and fax the music?

One Monday morning when I unlock the door to my office, the phone is already ringing wildly. At first, I don't understand a single word, I've never had a phone call from Japan, the line is bad, it's hard to get used to the accent of the English I'm hearing, and I haven't really arrived at my office at all yet. Quartet, visa, prison... all of a sudden, I understand only too well. On the Sunday, one of my quartets had travelled to Japan. They didn't have visas, they were detained at the airport, and were not admitted into the country. A gigantic misunderstanding: we actually *had* sent them the necessary visa papers, by registered post, to be sure that they didn't get lost. The addressee did indeed receive the notification from the postal service, but he had been worried that it was an unpleasant delivery and simply hadn't retrieved the letter. The consul was sent for, the minister of culture for the artists' home country was contacted, the day passed with frantic phone calls, and the quartet was released – two hours before their first concert.

Almost every time something like this happened, I had this odd experience that concerts that were preceded by a real or near-catastrophe would turn out to be particularly successful, even though the audience was not let in on any of the difficulties: that famous rush of adrenaline.

TRANSFORMATIONS

The more that 'professional' matters became routine, the more I turned my attention to the things not directly connected with concerts. In the early years of my career, I experienced some radical changes and quite a few crises, some less serious than others: changes in the line-up of some of my quartets, giving birth to my two children, and doing the splits between motherhood and the business. The LaSalle Quartet, which I had known ever since my childhood, the Cleveland Quartet, which I had handled for more than ten years, and the Brahms Quartett all disbanded, and my first marriage broke apart. New, younger quartets came along, and now I was the one they asked how to build a high-flying career. The things I'd learned from the older ones were to be passed on to the younger ones.

A few years later, I married again, outside the industry. No more rehearsals at home, no more quartet discussions at the kitchen table. Instead, there was a completely different discourse – seminars and psychoanalytical debates. I learned that the 'phenomenon' of the string quartet, beyond the music itself, attracted massive interest, sometimes downright inquisitiveness, even – and especially – among non-musicians.

In conversations with my husband, a psychoanalyst and an academic in the field of education, and with some of his colleagues, I found many

---

of the puzzles I experienced in my everyday professional life, as well as my attempts at understanding what my musicians were going through, being recast in a more precise vocabulary. All the little observations I had quietly accumulated over the years were, with the help of their questions, transformed into substantial descriptions.

Take, for example, the result of one heated discussion with friends, jotted down by my husband on a slip of paper:

- *Quartet players are not recognisable.*
- *The string quartet is the smallest possible form that allows individuality to transition into collectivity.*
- *Figures of speech about first and second violins*
- *The quartet and vocal ranges, the so-called natural ones: tenor, bass – soprano, alto*
- *(Instruments as imitators of the human voice); madrigal groups were the precursors of the quartet (maybe not historically, but logically).*
- *Genderless voice*
- *The quartet – like institutions generally – tends to be asexual (symbolically speaking, not in reality).*
- *Dyad*
  Trio
  Quartet: in the quartet, there's one too many.
- *Why have high-profile opera composers hardly ever written string quartets (Wagner, Verdi, Puccini) while composers who left an enormous body of string quartets wrote almost no operas (Beethoven, Schubert)?*
- *Is it possible to write both sacred music and string quartets?*
- *Was the quartet the specific invention of the emerging bourgeoisie that owned living rooms and drawing rooms but not vast palaces?*
- *Maybe the quartet is one subject but four individuals. (Who gives a*

quartet its name? Does it matter for the structure of quartets whether they take the founder's name or a collective name that has nothing to do with the name of any of the members? What sorts of names are used by quartets?)

- *The two violins are the problem. They get compared with each other (master-slave dialectic) but maybe they're still just one entity. Hence the bold conclusion: the quartet is actually a trio. However, because it's nonetheless a quartet, there's always a fifth, imagined position.*

When my husband handed me the slip of paper weeks later, I made a decision: I began to take notes everywhere. I scribbled down thoughts, however and wherever they came to me, I covered the backs of my notebooks and many loose sheets with writing, it was a complete mess. Notes I was looking for were nowhere to be found; others, forgotten long ago, resurfaced when I opened a drawer. Over time, out of the necessity of establishing some kind of order, and during conversations with both musicians and non-musicians, I slowly developed a sketch of the picture I would be able to paint, from my viewpoint as an observing and analytical fifth, close to, but not an integral part of my quartets.

- *What is a string quartet?*
- *How does a string quartet work?*
- *What kind of structure does it have?*
- *What about hierarchy, democracy, balance?*
- *How does a quartet decide its repertoire?*
- *What does daily life look like?*
- *What happens if someone leaves?*

OF ONE WHO WENT FORTH TO FOUND A STRING QUARTET

An enviable musical career awaited the highly talented young Viennese violinist Günter Pichler. At just eighteen years old, he had become the youngest leader of the Vienna Symphony Orchestra. Less than three years later, Herbert von Karajan summoned him to the Vienna Philharmonic Orchestra, also as leader. Besides Karajan, he played under Karl Böhm, Hans Knappertsbusch, Dimitri Mitropoulos and Leonard Bernstein, as well as Paul Hindemith, who was conducting his own opera, *Mathis der Maler*. In this internationally highly respected, very well-paid post, which would, without question, have soon led to a professorship at the Vienna conservatoire, Pichler would have been financially set – and completely secure – until the end of his days. Furthermore, with his talent and his position, he never lacked invitations to perform as soloist with other orchestras.

In record time, he had to learn the essential symphonic and operatic repertoire, as well as the great leaders' solos. But when the pressure eased and everyday routine set in, he realised that the only career move he could hope for would be to wait for his leader colleagues to retire so that he could become the top leader. Neither this prospect, nor his experiences as a soloist – for example, he once had to play fourteen different violin concertos within a period of a few weeks – fulfilled his ambitions or matched his dreams of how he wanted to make music. He left the orchestra and, with just a lectureship (no professorship yet) at the conservatoire (and with two children already!), he set out on a search for partners with whom he could found a string quartet. In Vienna, chamber music was highly respected, but not as a full-time occupation. As a result, his decision was met with incomprehension and horror. It took him no less than seven years to find three musicians who were as committed to playing string quartets as he was. With Klaus Maetzl (later Gerhard Schulz), Hatto Beyerle (later Thomas Kakuska and then Isabel Charisius) and Valentin Erben, he formed the quartet that ultimately became the Alban Berg Quartett. (For a brief period at the beginning, it was called the Schönberg Quartett.)

From a letter from Günter Pichler to Walter Levin, founder and leader of the LaSalle Quartet, publicly read out on the occasion of Levin's eightieth birthday, 6 December 2004, in Badenweiler:

Dear Walter

On your eightieth birthday, you're staying with our dear friend Klaus Lauer at his Römerbad Hotel in Badenweiler. What's taking place here this weekend is an extraordinary celebration for an extraordinary man. From the middle of the twentieth century on, so many things in the world of music would not have happened without you. Without you, the LaSalle Quartet – with all due respect to your colleagues – would not have become the LaSalle Quartet (although Evi[6] contributed to it, just as she has contributed to everything and still does). Without you, the music world would be the poorer by many important works; without you, there would not be such an encouraging number of excellent young quartets.

---

6 Evi Levin, wife of Walter.

The history we share began in Vienna, in 1970: the 'LaSalle' played a
Viennese School[7] concert cycle in the Vienna Konzerthaus, which I, of
course, went to hear. After the last concert, I went to the green room, the
scores tucked under my arm. When I thanked you, you pointed at the
scores and said something very typical for you: 'I say, you can read
music?!' When I told you that we had just founded a quartet, you
immediately became interested, and you invited me for breakfast the
next morning. And this was why: on your initiative, the 'Friedländer
Fellowship' had been set up, which made it possible for you to invite us
to come to Cincinnati and study with you for nine months.

That it actually happened was down to our ingenuity in raising
additional money and in obtaining our leave of absence, etc. From the
LaSalle side, everything more or less depended on Evi. She wrote (by
hand!) the preparatory letters (from you, Walter, I have no more than
four lines in my archive!), she took care of four apartments for a total of
eleven people, including the children; she arranged – by canvassing her
friends – for crockery, cutlery, rugs, bedclothes, curtains, radio and TV,
pictures (we even had two original Miró prints!); she organised
kindergarten places, and – friends! At that time, before I got to know
Evi in Cincinnati, I thought: this woman is either not for real or an
angel. We called her 'Mother Earth.'[8]

Well, then the lessons started in the Levin house. At their core was the
relentlessly probing question: what were you thinking here? The most
important thing was to question tradition. And so, apart from giving us

---

7 There are two 'Viennese Schools' in music history. The first one is the classic
'school' around Joseph Haydn, Wolfgang Amadeus Mozart and Ludwig van Beethoven,
at the end of the eighteenth and the beginning of the nineteenth century. The Second
Viennese School is the group around Arnold Schönberg, Alban Berg and Anton
Webern in the beginning of the twentieth century. Günter Pichler refers here to the
Second Viennese School.
8 English in the original.

all that essential information and advice – for example what to look up where – the lessons ended up leading us in the right direction.

Of course, there were occasions that were less than pleasant. After interviewing me, some journalist coined the term 'Levin-storm'. But those weren't thunderstorms, they were the perennial questions you asked us, which we actually should have asked ourselves, and which sometimes took us to our limits.

Do you remember? We played the Schubert A minor quartet. Shortly after the beginning of the first movement, Schubert has a transition bar for the first violin, from minor to major. I did my best, with those few notes, to emerge from the darkness into the light ... but apparently, I failed. Because you said: 'Tell me, Günter, is that supposed to sound jolly?' Rather piqued, my reaction was: 'I might as well go home then.'

Another example: Webern's Five Pieces, opus 5. Of course, we did our best to have good intonation. But you, unfortunately, were not happy.

Günter: 'I'm already struggling with the unnatural dynamics.'

Walter: 'Do you want to play Webern or not?'

Something very important you said, which I never tire of repeating: when I told you how disappointed I was that the Vienna Konzerthaus cycle planned for after our return would take place in the Schubert Hall and not in the Mozart Hall, you told me: 'Günter, it doesn't matter where you play, the important thing is how you play.'

CHAMPAGNE AND
MOZART K 421

*It was Alexander Schneider, the second violinist of the Budapest
Quartet, who gave us the idea. All four of us were at the Marlboro
Festival, and we'd already played together a lot in different
combinations. Sascha [Alexander] said: 'You're actually a good
team, the four of you. Why not form a quartet?' We thought that
wasn't a bad idea and sat down to play as a quartet with each
other for the first time. Mozart's D minor string quartet K 421.
It went well and felt right, and so we decided to give it a try. There
was a birthday party in my house in Vermont, Rudolf Serkin and
Alexander Schneider joined us, and there was champagne. And
that was how the Guarneri Quartet came into being.*

That's how, rather laconically, cellist David Soyer told me the story of the
birth of the Guarneri Quartet: Arnold Steinhardt, John Dalley, Michael
Tree and David Soyer.

I had never thought much about the name of the Guarneri Quartet.
One day Dr Willnauer, the head of the culture department of the
chemical and pharmaceutical company Bayer Leverkusen, gave me a
gift to pass on to the quartet – a concert poster for a 'Guarneri Quartet'
dating from the thirties. When I gave the poster to Arnold Steinhardt

and his colleagues, they told me that their name had been suggested by their mentor and teacher, Boris Kroyt, during the Marlboro Festival. In the thirties, he had been the viola player in a Guarneri Quartet in Europe (with Daniel Karpilowski, Maurits Stromfeld and Walter Lutz), which had been forced to dissolve into the diverging fates of four emigrants. Boris Kroyt ended up in the USA, where he joined the Budapest String Quartet (with Joseph Roisman, Alexander Schneider and Mischa Schneider), which had had to emigrate, too. With the name that had been suggested to them, the young Guarneri Quartet had inherited a bag full of history.

Arnold Steinhardt, first violinist of the Guarneri Quartet, dedicates an entire chapter of his book, *Indivisible by Four*, to the genesis of the quartet. For him, this story necessarily includes all the detail of how the four members came together over the course of several years, and of the various peculiarities of their different characters. Although he and David Soyer describe the beginnings in quite different ways (they would probably describe anything to do with the quartet in quite different ways), both mention Mozart's String Quartet in D minor K 421 – and champagne – as elements that sealed the deal. According to David Soyer, they played first and drank afterwards; according to Arnold Steinhardt, they drank first and then played. What they describe in a similar way, though, are their feelings while they played the Mozart quartet, from which the decision arose to share their future. David, rather plain and crisp, writes: 'It went well and felt right,' while Arnold writes: 'I had a feeling of arriving home, of absolute rightness.' So they had arrived where they belonged, and all four of them turned everything they had achieved so far upside down in order to take on the adventure of becoming a string quartet. At the time, Arnold Steinhardt was concert master of the Cleveland Orchestra, a secure, brilliant position, which he quit. Michael Tree – who until then had made his living as an excellent and much sought-after freelance violinist – switched to the viola, as if this had always been his destiny. They knew that they would have to travel a long way from the moment of their decision to their first concert, without any guarantee of a successful future. History tells us now that this future was to be illustrious.

Arnold Steinhardt writes:

The average concert-goer might think that a soloist can express, unfettered, his true artistic impulses in the concerto literature, but I found in these concerts that an orchestra, even the best of orchestras, is a very large creature that speeds up, slows down, and makes cumbersome twists and turns. Playing with Szell and the Cleveland had spoiled me, for they somehow made the elephant seem more like a gazelle. Elsewhere, I often had to follow rather than lead, and many times such a gulf opened up between the conductor's and the soloist's conceptions that the one or, at maximum, two allotted rehearsals hardly seemed sufficient to work out a satisfying interpretation. How different in chamber music, where you had some control over the people you played with and the amount of rehearsal needed! In a quartet one could, for better or worse, be totally responsible for the artistic results.

THE STRING QUARTET
AS A GENRE

––––––––

The only genre that has continuously maintained an unrivalled and central role in the evolution of classical music – dating back to around 1770 – has been the string quartet.

Bernard Fournier writes in his book *L'esthétique du Quatuor à cordes*: ' ... some 150 years after the emergence, in about 1600, of the string instruments of the violin family, we have the genius of one man in particular, Joseph Haydn, to thank for the birth and development of a genre that very quickly became an intellectual, aesthetic and also spiritual ideal for all those who engaged in it – the composer, the artist and the audience.'

The combination of instruments is strictly prescribed: two violins, one viola and one cello; one and the same sound texture. Strictly speaking, a formation of, for example, one violin, one viola, one cello and one double bass would also be a string quartet. However, the term is considered to denote the classic formation, and any other combination of instruments needs to be specified in the title. The range of means at the disposal of composers appears to be rigid and limited. But it's exactly this asceticism that seems to have fascinated many of them, and to have incited them to push against boundaries, to multiply sounds, to invent new ones and to exhaust the entire spectrum of expression from the

––––––––

perfect, quiet unison to the quasi-orchestral explosion. It seems that the motivation is not the instrument, but rather the writing, the language, and therefore the voice, or more precisely, the voices – in their relation to, with, and between each other.

'History shows,' Bernard Fournier continues, 'that most of the musicians who undertook to think about writing music in a radical way, and who went on to question their own aesthetic conceptions, turned to the string quartet at least at some point in their careers. Depending on the individual case, they drew from it energy or revitalisation, a focus of thought or a vision of the future. Thus, they contributed to the evolution of the genre, integrating modifications of language according to their own style, moulding the zeitgeist of their own age.'

In other words, string quartet music doesn't emerge from any fashion; it's not a trend. It is much more a place for research and experiment, to which almost all composers retreat when they want to reinvent or expand musical 'language', whether in general or simply their own. Composers explain that writing a string quartet is the greatest challenge for them. You often read in composers' reflections on their own works that the string quartet is closely connected to their inner lives, to the experiences that were elemental in terms of emotion for them. I asked the German composer Wolfgang Rihm whether he could write to me about what made him compose string quartets: he replied that it would be easier for him to write a new string quartet than to answer this question.

Bernard Fournier, in his book, describes the alluring charm that comes from what might seem to be the frugality and rigour of this most intimate form of making music, the essence of which is the subtle musical dialogue between the instruments. Within this asceticism, detail becomes the essential element that creates meaning. The result resembles not so much an oil painting in all its vibrant splendour, but rather a dense text, which, not unlike a complex philosophical essay, requires several readings, during which, again and again, new 'sentences' and 'thoughts' seem to emerge. This is where another dimension is added to the creative work of the individual: interpretation, which is tantamount to translation. Unlike a literary work, which anyone can read by themselves – as long as it is available as a book – music requires interpreters who create a connection between the author (composer) and the reader (listener). In the case of the string quartet, it requires four interpreters who have to agree on a translation/interpretation.

Fournier again: 'The secret of the string quartet is hidden behind this very simple reality: four instruments from the same family, similar and complementary, are put together in such a way that they become one.' As disarmingly simple as this sounds, the reality of it is complex – with every instrument comes a musician, a human being. The instruments cannot unite by themselves. Their sound can merge only through those who play them. But in the four human beings, the similarity and complementarity mentioned above are not necessarily a given as they are in their instruments.

Walter Levin comments:

For God's sake! If they play like one instrument, we don't need four of them! If we engage and pay four instruments, I want to hear four of them, not as one instrument, but as four distinct instruments. Differentiation of the voices, transparency of sound, clarity: all this comes first for me – no blurriness. It's of great importance to me that one hears everything that's written in the score, not just what's on the surface. You can compare it to a pianist who uses too much pedal. You can almost always recognise a quartet that has studied with me. Evi is able to tell me straight away, after listening to just two bars, whether someone studied with me. I often ask her: 'Why are you saying this?'

I don't think what they're doing is good.' She replies: 'Good or not good, that doesn't have anything to do it. It's how they're playing, that's what they've learned from you, no one else plays this way.' There are certain characteristics or criteria people learn from me, and that's not much of a mystery – you can name them. For me, there's a strong rhythmical component to the fore, the inner pulse, which is always perceptible, and which contains a certain forward motion. Things never stand still. That doesn't mean that the tempos are faster or slower, but that they have direction. Works go from the beginning to the end of a movement, or from the beginning to some other place, but they go somewhere. You immediately hear this relentless drive. Part and parcel of this inner rhythmical structure, of the pulse within, is a certain transparency of texture. What happens in a piece? Most string quartet compositions have a lot of inner space, not just a top and a bottom. At the bottom there's the bass, on top there's the melody, but in the middle – what's in the middle? That's where the harmony is, that's where imitations, contrasts, principal voices and accompanying voices are hidden – and I want to hear all of it!

And by the way, now I come to think of it, anything I have to say about music doesn't apply to just music.

More than a decade – and a whole generation – later, Raphaël Merlin, cellist of the Quatuor Ébène, emphasises the relationship between the string quartet genre and democracy:

In music, the problem of being four monodic instruments can, from a technical point of view, be explained well enough: the entire language of Western music rests fundamentally on the perfect chord of three tones (major or minor). As soon as polyphony brings in a fourth voice (as, for example, in the madrigals of the Italian Renaissance) the problem of doubling is posed. In other words, the problem of squaring the circle. From five voices on up, you're in the realm of an orchestra, and that's a different problem altogether – but at least an orchestra can quite organically follow the path determined by the absolute majority.

With four, democracy is difficult, but the quartet is well and truly the embodiment of the ideal – if only in the historical context of its creation. Freedom, listening, shared identity, shared ownership, interdependence: it's all there, like it is between the four iconic characters of the social revolution, Count and Countess Almaviva, Figaro and Susanna, born in the same period as the string quartet genre. Everyone needs everyone, and this little society finds itself under a magnifying glass in the middle of the search for a new model of justice. Three cheers for the Enlightenment, which gave the second violin and the cello a voice, too!

UNITY

___

Here is the truly phenomenal thing: the way in which – by music and through music – four fundamentally different people can conjure a unity, with all the nuances that are possible in music and between people.

Each member of the quartet [says Günter Pichler] *has to be as adaptable as a chameleon, able to adopt any possible colour – warm, vibrant, gaudy, soft, muted or cold – or rather, able to present himself in every possible colour. He has to be able to play fast or slow or loud or quiet and any degree in between, put simply, he must have complete command. Each member – I keep talking about mutual respect – has to be so good that he not only has qualities that the others admire or consider very good, but must also accept the weaknesses that each person has as well. This comprises the essence – to this, add the spirit of the individual player.*

It's all about picking the colours from the four individual palettes that promise to be powerful and iridescent in the ensemble, about defining the colour chart that is specific to the quartet – the Artemis Quartett calls it the DNA. One could – putting it very simplistically – imagine the process as follows. The individual musical qualities of the four musicians are inventoried and sorted into categories: those that are going to develop in their individuality even more passionately inside the quartet; some that have to be adapted to the group; and still others that will need to be contained, or even abandoned, within the constellation of the quartet. However, the parameters change with each new work in the repertoire, with each composer, with each new style or creative period. The characteristics of the sound and the challenges for the musicians are different in Wolfgang Amadeus Mozart or Joseph Haydn to those in Béla Bartók, Alban Berg or Wolfgang Rihm or Jörg Widmann.

Sorting and selecting means at the same time excluding; it means that some things are considered unsuitable for the common cause. What's left out won't disappear; it stays present in each player, lying in wait (sometimes treacherously) for its moment. A surprise package that makes your heart skip a beat (or causes a flood of adrenaline) during a concert, or that provokes a bitter argument at the most inconvenient moment. A quartet's playing depends on what has been achieved through meticulous work and by precise agreement, but also on the unpredictable little antics of any one of its members.

A short scenario (which is, of course, fictitious and would be rejected by any professional string quartet as completely unthinkable): the score of one of the pieces in today's concert programme requires that the violist begins a certain movement all by himself. In this moment, he has all the power. Hypothetically speaking, he could dictate the tempo (actually, it's the composer who prescribes the tempo!). The others would have to follow as if it was exactly what everyone had intended all along. Thinking about the range of possibilities here is, depending on your mood, either amusing or terrifying.

It requires enormous discipline and a cultivated balance of modesty and self-confidence to submit to the process – at times painful – of agreeing, and to uphold the agreement beyond the rehearsals. It's only by doing this, though, that an individual musician can, despite all the inherent restrictions of quartets, adapt to the group without completely assimilating. Unlike a soloist, who gives his all in a performance and justifiably expects the conductor and the orchestra to follow him, a quartet player is allowed only to give all that's appropriate for the quartet. Even in the heat of the moment (of the concert) he can't let himself go: he has to be able to hold back without closing himself off from the moment's inspiration. Not being allowed to be all you are inevitably produces frustrations and constraints, resulting in continual – and sometimes even explosive – friction. On the other hand, it does prevent stagnation and the creep of routine.

'During the first ten years of your career,' says Eugene Drucker, violinist of the Emerson Quartet, 'you work as a quartet mainly on playing as homogenously as possible. For the next ten years, you're busy learning to play heterogeneously, too.'

I asked Ori Kam, Jerusalem Quartet viola, for his view on the tension between freedom and peer pressure inside a string quartet. This is what he replied:

For me, a string quartet sits at the very edge between individual expression and teamwork. It is the largest ensemble where the members can still maintain their individual voices. This means that every member of a quartet fulfils every possible role: melody, countermelody, bass, harmony, texture, etc. In addition, a group of four encompasses a surprisingly large number of possible combinations: 1–1–1–1 (fugue), 1–3 (melody with accompaniment), 2–2 (canon). Changes between these can happen within a single bar. I like to think of playing in a quartet as an exercise in 'Ego management'. Each member must possess the self-awareness to consciously adjust who they are vis-à-vis the others, but also in relation to the music itself.

We are four strong personalities, opinionated and passionate. Yet I can't remember a moment where these traits got the upper hand over our commitment to the honest execution of the score. I think we direct most of our personalities into our sound. We spend the majority of our rehearsal time on issues pertaining to sound, such as carefully balancing the different voices, or finding the right timbre to express the emotional narrative in the music as we perceive it. Beyond dynamic markings, composers write few directions on what kind of sound to make. This leaves us free to express ourselves, while maintaining the highest level of transparency in executing the score to the best of our understanding. Scrupulously realising the score and expressing oneself freely seem to be two opposing things, yet doing both at the same time is the key ingredient for outstanding performances. I remember playing the Brahms Clarinet Quintet at the Schubertiade with my sister Sharon once, where we managed to perfectly build the structure of the first movement. The music reached a single, powerful climax at the peak of the development section. The effect was electric, and the five of us came off the stage in a trance.

I WISH I HAD THIS FREEDOM

'I wish so much that my colleagues, just once, would let me have that much freedom!' This was Günter Pichler's wistful sigh after listening to the trio – the middle part – of the third movement of Joseph Haydn's String Quartet op. 76/1, in which the first violin plays a cantilena, supported only by pizzicato in the other three instruments. A comment I never forgot.

Günter loved to tell me about teaching string quartets at the conservatoire in Cologne, and was always keen to hear about new young ensembles. And so I had sent him a copy of a recording of the Carmina Quartet that had been made during the first 'Premio Paolo Borciani' string quartet competition, held in 1987 in Reggio Emilia, Italy. Followed with great interest by the entire string quartet world, the competition had been set up in memory of Paolo Borciani, the colourful first violinist of the Quartetto Italiano.

The cast of the jury read like a kaleidoscope of string quartet playing styles of the eighties: Walter Levin (LaSalle Quartet), Elisa Pegreffi (Quartetto Italiano), Hatto Beyerle (Alban Berg Quartett), Norbert Brainin (Amadeus Quartet), Milan Škampa (Smetana Quartet), Sadao Harada (Tokyo String Quartet), and Valentin Berlinsky (Borodin Quartet).

No first prize was awarded. The laboriously negotiated result was a single second prize for the Carmina Quartet from Switzerland. No third prize was awarded either. Almost every single musical performance prompted controversy – sometimes heated. Only the Carmina Quartet's interpretation of the String Quartet op. 76/1 of Joseph Haydn was spontaneously and unanimously considered captivating.

I thought that the wistfulness I was inclined to hear in Günter Pichler's comment on the recording expressed something very characteristic about life in a string quartet. I had quite often detected a similar kind of wistfulness among string quartet musicians – at times in just a glance, or a half-remark, or in the smallest hint. Seventeen years later, I asked Günter Pichler whether he would allow me to quote his comment and name him. To my amazement, he remembered exactly both the Haydn recording and his reaction to it. He approved my request, but after a little reflection, he added that it wasn't really that his colleagues had been holding him back. As much as the Carmina way of playing had struck him as appealing when he had listened to the tape, it wasn't compatible with the style of the Alban Berg Quartett. Now there was no wistfulness any more. Rather, there was a feeling of pride, of having been able to let go of a possible interpretation because it wouldn't have been appropriate for his quartet, even though it had seemed to him at the time that it would suit him personally.

My first impulse was to discard as a misapprehension the wistfulness that I had ascribed to Günter Pichler and generally to all string quartet musicians: to replace the image of the suffering and repeatedly frustrated quartet member with one of a confident musician who, upon reflection, always gives priority to the quartet over himself. But this radical turnaround seemed questionable as well, and I ended up with the more complicated conclusion that maybe both versions were true.

THE SECRET

Organisational matters are often discussed during rehearsal breaks. As a result, I sometimes find myself talking with individual quartet members right after rehearsals. A quartet's private practice room is no concert hall, with its stage and appropriate measure of air and sound capacity; instead, these rooms are usually straightforwardly too small for all the energy and tension that builds up over hours within them. Generally, the question of the rehearsal room poses an enormous problem, especially for young quartets in big cities. Their own, mostly small, flats are not suitable for rehearsals – the neighbours! Other rooms in big cities are rare and expensive. Which leaves benefactors and imagination, for example a converted garage, a room offered by a Protestant community, a floor in an un-let office building. So many times, I would be told about the fresh frustration after a rehearsal in such a place, combined with the explosive news that things can't carry on like that, that the particular player talking to me would be looking as soon as possible for a teaching or an orchestral post, and anyhow, would be taking on another profession and turning his or her back on the quartet once and for all. A barrage of grumbles about one player or another, ostentatious sighs about how unbearable everything was. Over the years, I learned that a real split is never announced with a fanfare, and that eruptions of this sort are a natural result of close proximity and of this way of working. For people whose everyday life and professional focus involves literally sitting together in harmony, discord is inevitable. In a sense, it's the only way of avoiding suffocation.

Rehearsals during concert tours, which are naturally directed towards the upcoming concerts, are subject to even more tension. For example, one individual player might think the repertoire to be performed is, objectively speaking, 'stage ready', or alternatively still needs tweaking, or reworking – while the others disagree with equal certainty. Or perhaps everyone is struggling with their own stage fright and feeling either at one with or alien to the others. Or maybe someone, on a given day, feels a deep aversion – justified or not – to someone else – or to everyone else – in the quartet. Nerves are exposed, a light remark can get misunderstood as a fundamental criticism or as calling everything into question. Trivialities that have nothing to do with music can get out of control and cause terrible arguments, and, more often than not, petty stuff provides a welcome vent for pent-up nervousness.

The clarinettist and composer Jörg Widmann, who once joined a quartet for a performance of the Brahms Clarinet Quintet, describes it like this: 'We rehearsed the quintet as the last piece before the concert. We had to leave the stage at half past seven, because the audience was let into the hall, and I went with the quartet to our joint green room. Within minutes, I had to run away – almost literally. I felt like a voyeur.'

Every quartet has its own way of dealing with this kind of tension. Some go completely silent, refusing to talk to each other, others argue or crack jokes. Some avoid each other, others seek each other's presence. Old hands among the nervous go for victims other than their quartet colleagues: it might be that the lighting isn't right and the lighting manager is nowhere to be found, or perhaps there is an error showing up in the printed programme which is worth a noisy fuss, or maybe the chairs are too low or creak. The others, old hands too, dig themselves into their green rooms and practise as loudly as possible.

Right before the performance starts, unity gets restored – what matters now are their joint and personal aspirations. The feelings, the innermost fears of each, become palpable for each of the others, are completely exposed to them. The atmosphere crackles with the emotional charge. Immediately before going on stage is the most intimate moment, the most vulnerable – they are laying themselves out ready, in the hope that the spark ignites, the spark that matters so much both to the artists and to the audience. The unification happens publicly, on stage: they put their bows on the strings and begin to play. There's no alternative: it's either the four of them or nothing. From the first step on to the stage, they are relying on each other, on what they as artists respect and love in each other. They are relying on being able to inspire and carry each other along. After a performance of the Brahms Quartet op. 67 with its beautiful viola theme, the first violinist confesses: 'Each and every time, I love listening to him [his colleague] so much that I almost miss my entry!'

The life and work of a string quartet are like a permanent ridge walk. First the narrow path leading up, and then the narrow crest along which the four of them have to walk, roped together as a team. Whoever steps out of line will pull all the others into the abyss. This is true on stage as well as in life. Every single concert is, every time, a fresh expression of enormous discipline by all four of them. The history of the quest for the collective statement is kept hidden from the audience, but its drama is conveyed, by and through the music. A soloist plays openly and directly to the audience, almost always standing facing out towards them. The musicians of a string quartet are seated almost opposite each other, in a more-or-less open semicircle. They are playing to each other, and at the same time for an audience that is watching and listening to a highly concentrated process of unification.

The amphitheatre is both a closed system and an open system [Raphaël Merlin comments]. *This semi-circular space should be used as a whole, with the physical positioning being, at the same time, symbolic positioning. If one member always gets carried away by the forward momentum in the tempo, then another will eventually take up the position of defender of the just cause of the still moment of listening. It's an interdependence born from experience, which can be shed pretty quickly if we find ourselves playing with other musicians, or as soloists: but for right now, we understand that we've arrived at the point where our position in the quartet completely defines us; that we have evolved from autonomous individuals into quarters of a whole.*

During a summer string quartet masterclass, one student quartet performed a movement of Beethoven. Immediately afterwards, the teacher asked for the lights to be switched off. It was a complete blackout. The teacher said nothing while silence fell, and darkness penetrated every pore. Once the atmosphere had turned electric with a mixture of anticipation, even fear, the teacher asked the musicians to play the movement again. They started out tentatively, trying to find each other in the darkness. He had them repeat the first bars, several times, and suddenly, something was released. Everyone knew their part, and they knew each other. Without the support of the music stand in front of them, all that was left to them was confidence in themselves and in each other. In this moment, I, as a listener, thought I sensed some of the secret.

The cellist Sonia Wieder-Atherton has often played with string quartets, although she has never been a quartet member herself. Despite – or even because – of this, I have had long conversations with her about this phenomenon, which she describes as specific to string players. One day, after her pianist, due to illness, had to pull out of several of their recitals together, her violinist colleague Raphaël Oleg stepped in. Without further ado, the programme was changed, and violin/cello duo recitals were scheduled instead. After one of the concerts, she wrote to me:

This level of concentration, of understanding the risks you can take, and, above all, the deep knowledge of each other which stems from years of playing together – even if it was sporadic – all of this is beyond the realm of what you can express with words. Despite being enormously tired, even frightened, we had a wonderful time. I felt those many hours of work we had shared – a powerful bond. I've worked a lot with the piano and a lot with the violin, and I've always thought to myself that it's different between string players. So, I had to think of our conversation about the string quartet. It's yet another dimension of knowing each other, almost animal. I can feel exactly, I can measure the inner ease (or unease) of the violinist when he puts his bow on the string, and I'm sure that he senses exactly the same from me. I know intuitively how long each note is going to be, whether it will end at the tip of the bow or not, whether it's going to be fast with a light pressure on the string, or long, with a heavy bow. The bond, the understanding, with my pianist, is very strong, too, musically speaking, but it's different. Among string players, there's this something, the animal, that actually makes the relationship more complicated. It introduces something that's passionate, relentless, reckless, almost violent. (And I'm not talking about a romantic relationship!)

A MALE PRESERVE?

———

It became apparent early on that the string quartet was not necessarily a male thing – and this was at a time when orchestras were still almost exclusively male preserves. Since then, the generational change of guard in orchestras has meant that quite often – and more often, the further north in Europe you go – orchestras hire more women than men. But back to string quartets. In the sixties, Elisa Pegreffi, for example, was second violin in the Quartetto Italiano, and in the seventies Martha Katz was the viola in the Cleveland Quartet. By the 1980s, there were successful all-women quartets, such as the Lafayette Quartet from Canada, or the Vertavo String Quartet from Norway.

In my early years as a string quartet agent, however, I represented only men's string quartets – not by conscious decision, but because the top-ranking ensembles represented by Konzertdirektion Schmid at the time happened to be men-only. I guess this had an enormous effect on my conception of the string quartet. It was only when the Carmina Quartet from Switzerland – made up of two men and two women – won the first Borciani string quartet competition in 1987 that I became familiar with a mixed line-up. As it happened, another completely new thing for me was that we – the Carmina and I – were part of the same generation. Until then, all my quartets had been at least one generation

———

older than I was. It took me a while to get over my initial feeling that this was strange (perhaps you could also say to overcome my prejudices).

Seeing a mixed quartet line-up on stage was new to me – as it was for many in the audience. But there were other confusing innovations, too. The colours, for example! Before then, there were no surprises – string quartet musicians would come on stage in black and white, wearing tails and white shirts, one quartet the same as another. Then, suddenly, long colourful dresses jumped out at you. And then there was this new attitude of the men upon entering and leaving the stage: always politely yielding to the ladies, in the manner of perfect gentlemen. In my experience up to that point, string quartet players had not been remarkable for their chivalrous behaviour!

At the time, in my routine work with the Carmina Quartet, I just acted (or reacted) with my existing tool kit. I didn't spend too much time wondering about the character of the balance within the quartet, or what specific characteristics might come from the fact that the quartet consisted of two women and two men, and that two of the members were married to each other (first violinist Matthias Enderle and violist Wendy Enderle were already married when the quartet was founded).

It wasn't until much later that I began to take a closer look, and to try and understand why things were the way they were. I wondered whether I could recognise any patterns in the way quartets were put together – in the hope, perhaps, of being able to offer the odd piece of practical advice for dealing with the kinds of crises that seemed to be normal in 'mixed cast' situations. What mattered here was not only the 'stage impression', but also – and even more importantly – what could be gleaned from the petty (or not so petty) stuff of everyday life.

And I, too, am a different person today. My way of looking at things has changed over the decades and throughout the course of my life. When I started out, I was twenty or more years younger than my artists.

Today, I am twenty or more years older than them, and I see many things from a certain distance, cushioned by years of experience. And so, these days, I allow myself to make some claims that are not necessarily scientifically proven, but are the considered product of experience. And I give myself licence to express preferences that might not come across as politically correct.

For example, I love the cast of four men. It harbours a tremendous – at times raw – energy and power. I ascribe this to the fact that talking about problems and sensitivities is not necessarily the greatest of male talents, and so every single friction – in fact, the entire potential for conflict – gets poured, unfiltered, into the musical mixture. The 'wrangling' has almost always miraculously evaporated by the time playing is over – the energy remains.

In a cast of four women, I have observed exactly the opposite. Each nuance of atmosphere, each minute dissonance, has to be settled by discussion, and will be discussed for as long as is required to get to the bottom of it. Nothing remains bottled up. And so, the playing of the music reflects a consensus that has been achieved down to the very last detail.

The combination of one woman and three men, a relatively common one in recent years, is, in my opinion, the most stable formula for a quartet – for the time being at least, probably the ideal one. Here, the woman is the queen, even if in everyday life this is not visible from the outside. There is also a certain eroticism here, which can be transmitted to the audience. I often have the impression that the woman, by just being a woman, evokes the best in the three men, who 'behave' in her presence, reining themselves in before things get too rough.

Raphaël Merlin of the Quatuor Ébène has told me that internal relationships in the quartet improved vastly when the violist Marie Chilemme joined the quartet. A little ironically, he comments on her influence on the quartet's grand Beethoven project of 2019: 'I don't even want to try to imagine how we would have coped with the Beethoven cycle with Mathieu or Adrien; there would have been blood on the walls!'

Oddly enough, until the last change of personnel in the Artemis Quartett, I'd never worked with a quartet of three women and one man. So, at the time of writing, it is still too early for me to spot the ways the energies flow, or to name any particular opportunities or risks this combination brings.

The string quartet is, after all, a mirror of society, when it comes to gender as with everything else. Which is why today, it's no surprise any more to find one or more women playing in a professional string quartet. And yet, on the professional circuit, male (or male-dominated) quartets are still the majority. This has less to do with any questioning of whether women are 'capable' of making long-term commitments than it does with priorities, which inevitably shift when starting a family. Even though today's fathers, encouragingly, are very often present or even downright motherly, the fact remains that it is easier for a father to live the life of a travelling musician than for a mother.

The stress of being a travelling musician and a mother at the same time takes a huge toll on a woman, both physically and mentally. Most often, it's another family member who makes it possible for her to be a 'travelling mother' – it could be a grandmother who accompanies her on tour, or grandparents living nearby who offer the child or the children a second home. Sometimes it is the husband who puts his own career on the back burner and keeps day-to-day life going – something that's not so rare today. Whatever the set-up, a family life of this kind demands a lot from everyone, and it is such good luck when it works out.

This having to juggle is not specific to string quartets. It happens to any female musician who doesn't play in an orchestra close to home with regular working hours, and to anyone who has to go 'on tour' to practise their profession. Things may be easier to manage for famous soloists, because they are more likely to be able to afford the enormous financial outlay involved in taking a child plus helper with them on tour. All too often, for chamber musicians, it means there are times when they pay more for giving concerts than they earn.

But what does this kind of 'extension' of one quartet member mean for the balance within the quartet? A pregnant colleague is never – as far as I have ever noticed – a problem. But it is hard to predict what it will be like to go on tour with the young mother, plus her child, plus their supporting person. It is hard to foresee the extent to which everyone will become a co-parent. It is not up to the young mother alone to get fit for the concerts; it's up to everybody. It is everybody's job to collectively manage the rehearsals and the travelling in a way that ensures that maximum concentration can be summoned up for the concert. It requires a high amount of tolerance and, above all, a great deal of empathy – from the colleagues as well as from the concert organisers.

Amongst concert organisers, meanwhile, things have also changed. These days, you come across many young parents working with organisers who are fathers and mothers themselves, and so are more mindful of the concerns of artists travelling with their babies than were their counterparts in earlier years. As a result, they offer help with a lot of imagination and practical creativity, for example through networks of experienced multilingual babysitters.

In my eyes, one of the most interesting situations in a quartet is when there is a couple in the group. It was there quite early on: for example in the Quartetto Italiano, in the Cleveland Quartet, and, as I mentioned before, in the Carmina Quartet. Nowadays, this phenomenon is surprisingly common (see the Pacifica Quartet, Pavel Haas Quartet, Belcea Quartet, Casal Quartet, Armida Quartet and many others). As far as I can tell, it doesn't make any difference if the match was made within the quartet or if the two musicians were already a couple when the quartet was founded. It's not so surprising that two musicians within a quartet should fall for each other, considering how closely linked the lives of individuals within the group are, and, ultimately, how little space tour life leaves for anything coming from the outside, or for anything new. Also, the emotions shared in the making of music – and in the travelling, with all its adventures – are particularly likely to bring people together. Is it possible that the fact so many couples are found within professional quartets these days has something to do with musicians quite often coming together and committing to their quartets at an extremely young age (some while still at music school, before their time at a conservatoire)? If they bind themselves so young, does the quartet become their home, in a particularly intense way?

The interplay of intimacy and alienation is particularly delicate in sibling quartets. If siblings grow up together playing quartets, they will at some point feel a need to distance themselves from one another. In their efforts to differentiate themselves within the framework of the quartet, they will seek an additional identity outside it, looking to become colleagues instead of siblings. It's a deliberate exercise of gaining an inner distance, which means no longer only interacting along the paths known to them since time immemorial. Ultimately, it's about discovering an unknown within what has always been familiar.

If married couples are involved, things get even more complicated. The fraught question of loyalties often pops up along the path from disagreement to eventual agreement: to whom is loyalty due, the partner or the quartet? Where would you rather fight it out – in the group or in your relationship? I have often wondered whether the two in a couple within a quartet end up having more than their fifty per cent of the votes, whether they exercise a kind of social superpower within the quartet, and whether, because of this, the quartet's balance – which is always precarious anyway – is jeopardised. But what I've observed is surprising. Instead of a kind of back-door supremacy for the couple, which I might have expected, what I've actually experienced more often is that coalitions put together for quartet matters are quite independent of family relationships. On the other hand, some annoying little idiosyncrasies of character can afflict the quartet less because they seem to be contained by the couple – they are neutralized inside the two-person relationship. And it's also true that the fact that two members of the quartet are officially 'responsible' for each other seems to disburden the other two. In any case, I've noticed time and again that a couple within the quartet provides it with a certain stability.

FOUR SOLOISTS,
FOUR TRIOS, SIX DUOS

From a rich collection of thoughts and reflections Raphaël Merlin sent to me:

A quartet is actually made up of four soloists (ABCD), but, even more so, of four trios (ABC, ACD, ABD, BCD) and of six duos (AB, AC, AD, BC, BD, CD). Each and every one of these configurations can, even in the most mundane of situations, very quickly bring about the exposure of different facets of a member's personality to the observing eyes of the other three. It's like a kaleidoscope that never stops rotating – each player presents differently, depending on whether he is with all three of the others, or with two of them, or with only one. Sometimes during these prismatic variations, character traits that are almost contradictory are revealed. Even if A and D end up in a massive argument during a rehearsal because they just cannot see eye to eye about intonation (an extremely complex topic, made even more complex since the so-called Baroque revolutions of the mid-twentieth century), these two musicians will still be able to ride the metro together in the most amicable, affectionate harmony. Away from the other two observers, any affront can evaporate without residue – the most acute professional conflicts need not affect the general camaraderie. But this

*game of abstraction doesn't always work. The whole challenge is to
know how to navigate the locks between the work arena on one level
and the garden of outside life on another.*

*If one member is unable to attend a rehearsal for family reasons or
because of illness, the three others who are keeping to the schedule will
of course indulge in a bit of biting of the fourth's back, but will also
find their interactions easier, because they are refreshed, even invigorated
by the empty fourth chair. This shifting of relationships is a real
phenomenon, manifesting itself in other situations, too: in the presence
of a fifth conspirator come to play quintets; with a listener from whom
we are seeking advice; or with any random person who inadvertently
steps into our closed society.*

*Like it or not, the quartet relationship generates great psychological
violence; it inexorably thrusts each member into a confidential, even
confessional kind of relationship with the other three. Because it's not
possible to share the mysteries of music without exposing oneself to the
glare of the group's spotlight, each member, even with the most innocent
grin or tiny comment, broadcasts his opinion, sometimes involuntarily,
on matters as crucially important as they are intimate. The
personalities involved end up weaving for themselves a network of
bonds that are totally laid open to the view. Extremely personal
decisions, about family, divorce, sometimes even about birth or
pregnancy, are subject to discussion, to approval, because the impacts on
the collective career are inevitable. This can sometimes come up against
the limits of your self-respect. Someone who just wanted to be supportive
can suddenly find himself the villain, while someone else who just
wanted to open up to the others might end up feeling like a victim.
The big problem – and also the very thing that holds the search for
excellence and for community together – can be summed up in one
word: interdependence. This interdependence is the price you pay for*

opening up the sanctuary of music, where playing is an act, if not of love, at least of reconciliation. How amazed we were when, after one of our most violent arguments – which took place in the sacristy of the small church of Santa Cristina d'Aro in Catalonia, only a few seconds before the performance – we found, in playing, an unhoped-for symbiosis, and a sharing of our relief.

THE PINNACLE?

————

'Chamber music' – these words act like a magic spell. Whenever any musician, whether an orchestral player, an amateur or one of the great soloists, speaks about chamber music, their eyes begin to sparkle. Nowadays, almost every orchestra has its own chamber music series, with concerts given exclusively by groups put together by members of the orchestra. Soloists meet like-minded colleagues at festivals to play chamber music. Sometimes they go on tour together afterwards, or even start their own chamber music festivals, to which they invite each other. Great moments of music are preserved for future generations from such festival concerts: piano trios, string trios, horn trios, oboe quartets, quintets, string sextets, septets, octets, nonets, wind quintets. Some are recorded in a studio, others with hidden microphones, without the knowledge of the players. The musicians involved already know each other, or they get to know each other. They come together, and they separate, promising to meet again, or not. Only one combination almost never appears in this spontaneous and transitory form: the string quartet.

The violinist Gidon Kremer, soloist and chamber musician, has been admired for decades as one of the great musicians of our time. This is how he reflects on the string quartet:

————

*The multi-layered character of musical expression in the quartet
corresponds to my idea of a model of life where polyphony and balance
– harmony – can meet. I see this not only as a reflection of the givens
of 'Being', but also as a pinnacle of our 'endeavour for solidarity and
betterment'. In the first place, there are – among other things – tension,
struggle, convergence and the joy of discovery, all of which are
psychologically, as well as instrumentally, in permanent flux. This
applies to Beethoven and Schubert as much as it does to Shostakovich,
Berg or Nono. The many examples, scattered across the centuries, of the
courage of composers in pursuing the theme of the string quartet in
their creations should very much encourage everyone to engage with it
– whether they are musicians (amateur or professional) or just people
who love music. There is hardly a more cogent example of 'living with
each other' in the history of civilisation. (How admirable are all those
quartet line-ups that, over decades, manage to keep their conversation
going!) Those who want to play string quartets cannot just flirt with
the idea. It demands everything from you, even if it's just for one piece.
The only way of doing it is to open yourself up and give yourself to
it entirely. The satisfaction waiting for you is overwhelming.*

Even Gidon Kremer never founded a string quartet, and only occasion-
ally performed a quartet in a chamber music programme. The string
quartet, he says, requires a commitment to a permanent line-up. This,
for him, has remained a terrain upon which he does not dare to venture.

The purist tenet that a string quartet should have absolute priority in
the lives of its members was easy for me to accept and to advocate in
my early years as a string quartet agent. The quartets for which I worked
at that time were embodiments of this principle. They were successful;
they had proved that it was indeed possible to have a social position
and a livelihood as a string quartet. They all earned a monthly salary

as professors or quartets in residence at colleges or universities. It was only when I began to work for younger quartets, for those who were just starting out, with no stable income and without professorships, that I realised, with embarrassment, the implications and even the arrogance of such glib assumptions. Professorships or lectureships for entire quartets are extremely rare in Europe, though commonplace in the US, and it remains highly unlikely that the four members of a string quartet could be professors at the same conservatoire. The prospects for a regular income sufficient to cover the bare necessities are bleak, for the younger as well as for the older string quartets. In view of this predictably precarious future, one wonders what makes young people decide to give it a try: to forgo security and embark on the adventure of a string quartet, even though, given their talent and their individual achievements and successes, they could perfectly well (or do already) enjoy a comfortable income and a secure position. Are they, as some people think, freaks, chasing an illusion?

DECISIONS

The decision to follow a career as a musician is made in early childhood. Inevitably, this is a family matter. A child can have many reasons for learning to play an instrument – if doing so is their choice. It might be down to the shape or particular sound of an instrument, a chance encounter with a piece of music, or with a person, or some concert experience. For the parents, going down this road means an enormous commitment: looking for the right teachers, appropriate schools, good instruments, and also, often, financial support. Some families undertake to move to a different city, so that the child is offered the right conditions. Without support from their parents or their families, for example because their talent has not been recognised, or because financial resources are lacking, even children of exceptional talent with an absolute determination to become musicians face a path of trial and tribulation. However the decision has been made – alone or collectively – the primary goal will not be to become a member of a string quartet. If a child studies the violin and is talented, you tell them about the great legends of the violin, you take them to hear the great soloists in concerts, or you get them CDs or videos of the artists. You point out role models like Jascha Heifetz or Yehudi Menuhin, Gidon Kremer or Maxim Vengerov, Lisa Batiashvili, Isabelle Faust or Hilary Hahn.

Only rarely do you point to Arnold Steinhardt, Günter Pichler, Norbert Brainin, Corina Belcea or Simin Ganatra, or even the violinists of the Guarneri Quartet, the Alban Berg Quartett, the Amadeus Quartet, the Belcea Quartet or the Pacifica Quartet. Mount Olympus is inhabited by soloists, not by string quartets.

Lukas Hagen, of the Hagen Quartet from Salzburg, remembers:

Of course, our parents – that is, our father – had something to do with us starting to learn to play instruments at all. What's more, he played Hausmusik [chamber music] *with us from the very beginning. From the time Clemens started playing the cello, we played quartets, too. Whatever our father did to make it work, we never felt forced. One reason could be that his initial idea was not for us to become professional musicians. He actually started to learn the violin along with me. But surely the decisive thing was the idea that we would make music together from the start. This was obviously more fun for us, and more motivating than having to practise our instruments all by ourselves.*

Although not initially intended by their father, the quartet became the centre of the careers of three of the Hagen siblings. In times when three-child families are considered large, family quartets are likely to remain an exception.

Only a few will be able to pursue a career as a soloist, so for most music students, an orchestra post will be the desired and honourable objective of their studies. An orchestra promises some kind of regular income, possibly even the social security benefits a country offers, and a pension (at least for now!) – and it brings with it a certain social status. Orchestral musicians typically don't have too much responsibility; they don't have to take care of planning concerts, organisational matters, music, stands or travelling. Those who are lucky enough to find a position in a financially secure orchestra are free to arrange their entire lives around the music if they wish. Whether they play tennis, teach, paint, devote themselves to the study of philosophy, or play string quartets in their spare time, is entirely up to them. Artistically speaking, too, the individual orchestra player has hardly any creative leeway (to be precise, this applies only to the strings). Before you are employed by an orchestra, it's explicitly soloistic skills that are demanded from you; but from then on, these are almost irrelevant, apart from the occasional solo if you are a section leader. A good orchestra is characterised, among other things, by a homogenous string sound. This requires the individual player to merge with the sound and at the same time to disappear in it. On questions of interpretation, the opinion of the individual player doesn't matter, either. It's part of one's duties to execute the conductor's intentions as faithfully as possible. The need for subordination, for conformity, and the lack of discussion about musical matters allow very limited room for enthusiasm and emotion – except where it concerns the mastering of one's own instrument. Within these narrow parameters, the musician is expected to deliver top-quality performance and, at the same time, to restrain his inner self. These contradictory expectations can result in a strong feeling of loneliness, which a committed musician may try to overcome – for example, by founding a string quartet.

So, the conclusion seems plausible that orchestras are ideal hotbeds for string quartets. With fifty or seventy string colleagues around, it shouldn't be too difficult to find three like-minded and socially acceptable partners with whom it would be possible to launch a string quartet. Especially since everyone has more or less the same work schedule, so the necessary regular rehearsals would be easy to arrange.

But orchestral musicians are not necessarily free to accept long-term engagements: they have ceded control over their time to the orchestra, and they can accept engagements only if these don't clash with rehearsal or concert schedules. Navigating the free concert market as an independent music group, in contrast, requires both the ability to commit and a good deal of flexibility, neither of which is really compatible with the cumbersome bureaucracy of a giant apparatus.

A soloist, on the other hand, doesn't seem to need to abide by any rules, can react spontaneously to any wishes or demands and can, theoretically, set their priorities regardless of others. While it's completely different from the loneliness of an orchestral musician, a soloist knows about loneliness, too, and might understandably develop a similar wish of uniting with others in a string quartet, as a way of preserving for themselves an oasis of togetherness. But a soloist is, practically speaking, just as inflexible and time-constrained as the orchestral musician. So, a quartet cannot be more than an affair of the heart, and will have to give way if and when a soloistic offer beckons.

Only a very few professional musicians come to the string quartet because they are inspired by hearing the music as children or as teenagers. It's mostly by happenstance or teacherly prescription. It can become a life-changing experience to discover what it's like when four players pass the ball to each other, when you inspire each other, and when your single voice – not very satisfying in your solitary practice – becomes an indispensable thread in the fabric of the ensemble.

REPUTATION

There's an aura of elitism and exclusivity around the string quartet, suggesting, according to the usual laws of the marketplace, an expensive business. One might expect a classy club behind the scenes. But, in reality, modesty prevails (when it comes to the ticket prices), and revenues from chamber music concerts, as well as the fees, are on the low side. Even if the reputation of a string quartet is comparable to that of a single soloist, the fees are lower. And while the income has to be divided by four, the costs quadruple: four instruments, five flight tickets (Mr. Cello needs a ticket of his own, if he is admitted to the cabin at all – which he might not be for security reasons), four hotel rooms, four sets of concert gear, two taxis (one taxi is not enough for four plus cello and luggage); the list could go on forever.

In spite of this, one finds, again and again, successful soloists, mostly violinists, founding their own string quartets and reserving entire blocks of dates in their otherwise packed diaries for their string quartet activities. They accept that the fee for the whole quartet will be at best about the same as the fee they normally earn on their own, just because they are appearing in a chamber music series instead of a solo recital series – which inevitably means a financial loss for them. And it's not only the size of the fees that differs, but also the way 'the artist' is perceived and treated. When the artist engaged by an organiser is a soloist, it's a single artist – in the case of a string quartet, it's no less than four. A soloist is regarded as a cherished guest, for whom you might want to make staying in a strange city as pleasant as possible, whom you welcome and court, more or less, depending on their degree of fame. You can't really *court* a string quartet. This 'artist' is perceived as an autonomous unit, self-sufficient, and in need of neither help nor attention – a far cry from any star cult or glamour.

For many decades, chamber music subscriptions series would sell out, and seats would even be passed on by inheritance. This picture has been changing faster and faster, a process that started in the mid-eighties. The mostly ageing audiences are dwindling; funding by city councils has been cut in the course of austerity measures. There are no more waiting lists for subscriptions. The private concert societies were never (and still aren't) professional or profit-oriented concert organisers. They are the work of doctors, pharmacists, lawyers or teachers, who take on the organisation of concerts in their spare time, and they normally don't have the means, the know-how or the time to recruit new audiences beyond their own circles. The gulf between the generations is still widening. Since the nineties, there has been a lot of talk about the dying of chamber music, and specifically of the string quartet. In contrast, the number of young people choosing the string quartet before they even finish their studies keeps on growing. When the Ariel Quartet registered at the Borciani competition in 2002, two of the members needed a signature from their parents because they weren't of age. Never, before the beginning of this century, have there been so many young quartets, and all of them must share the allegedly shrinking numbers of opportunities for concerts. There's no simple explanation for this. Is it the repertoire, or are they really attracted by the combination of low fees, critical audiences, and a boy scout lifestyle? Are these good reasons for this decision? If the prospects for a secure life are so bleak, and if the whole thing is only a fringe phenomenon, you might be allowed to ask: Why not choose the simpler solution, and regard the string quartet as an extra income, a side line, and look for – or keep – a secure employment?

But establishing an international stage career as a string quartet requires concentration, ambition, flexibility in terms of time, and spontaneity from every participant – to a degree that is just not possible when there are parallel obligations. There are prestigious exceptions: orchestra quartets, like the Gewandhaus Quartet or the Philharmonia Quartet, and soloists' quartets, like the Zehetmair Quartet or the Tetzlaff Quartet, seem to give the lie to the theory of necessary priorities, because they are successful. Nonetheless, it's musicians who have decided to make the quartet their first priority who really bear the brunt of preserving the concert series tradition.

FRIENDS?

It would be a romantic oversimplification to think of a string quartet as just a group of four friends who found each other through their love of chamber music. Such a thing would require a number of implausible coincidences, for example each of the four friends happening, by chance, to play the right instrument. A personal decision to form a quartet with three other people, or to join an existing quartet, is at the same time a decision to link your life with the lives of three other individuals – and to do so in a very intense way that extends well beyond the purely professional. Most of the twenty-somethings are fortunate enough not to foresee how comprehensively they will be sharing their lives, how deeply interwoven their individual spheres will be in the constellation of their quartet.

Becoming a member of a string quartet does not just require learning the relevant literature, listening to each other and playing music with each other – it is a whole way of life that expands human qualities and demands sacrifices. It allows for almost no routine, keeping everyone constantly on their toes. A shared everyday life develops that is comparable to no other: working on the music, emotions, stage fright, travelling together, ambition, fear of failure, discouragement, the joy of making music and of having success. Living as a quartet calls for a professional and economic companionship that reaches into and dominates the entirety of each individual life.

For example, where and how does a quartet live? A quartet doesn't only exist in its concerts and on tour, it requires a place where it can rehearse and work on a day-to-day basis. Which means that the musicians in a quartet must all have their homes, their day-to-day lives, in the same place. What if one has a relationship, and their partner gets a job in a different city that he or she can't or doesn't want to give up? Is it unavoidable that being a member of the quartet means deciding against the relationship?

Whoever joins an orchestra becomes part of a pre-existing, hierarchical institution, where artistic matters are strictly separated from administrative matters. Each administrative department employs people trained for their specific jobs with one well-defined role each. An orchestra board, consisting of elected members of the orchestra, mediates between the musicians and the management, and trade unions (separate unions for the musicians of the orchestra and for the administrative staff) ensure that the interests of the employees are respected. Everything is laid down: the level of duties, the size of salaries, the daily allowances, the category of hotels, the dress code. A quartet, in contrast, is neither a single person who can take decisions at will, nor a stable structure within an institution that prescribes everything. A quartet is not a company advertising its success with an army of employees and a city-centre office building. Nevertheless, a quartet earns a joint living – the four musicians do not earn money unless they perform together – and, through this, they become a single economic enterprise.

Sharing an economic basis like this results in something like an alignment of individual fates. The four musicians really do submit themselves to direct financial dependence on each other. The non-material union can then reveal its very mundane flipside, exposing completely different character traits in the individuals to those revealed in the music. (Not every great musician is, at the same time, a magnanimous person!) As long as they are students, there are hardly any differences. No one has any money. But a quartet doesn't develop as a commune or a kibbutz. The quartet members do their best to become a unity in music, and they also go to great lengths to coordinate their private and professional lives. But this doesn't mean that they must completely harmonise their private existences. With every step into a professional life, and with every stage of growing up, differences in character and social environment become more and more apparent. One has always been thrifty, careful and foresighted; another is a bon viveur, not caring too much about tomorrow. One starts a family and takes on responsibility; another remains single.

What happens if someone falls ill, falls in love or becomes pregnant? With every change in a player's personal relations outside the quartet – a new family, a private separation, a new house – his or her relationship to the quartet changes, too. The question of what significance the quartet has in a musician's life, and to what degree they devote themselves to the quartet, arises again and again over the course of their lives. The older the members of the quartet are, the smaller the number of options. The transition from the age when everything still seems possible to the age when doors slowly begin to close is arguably the most critical time for a string quartet. It's the time when any decision in favour of the quartet is made very consciously, taking absolutely everything into account.

Career progress manifests itself in the number and the standard of concerts, and in an improvement in the economic situation. You might expect that the state of that progress would play an important role in coping with conflicts, that it would sharpen them or take away their sting. Of course, success and failure do shape the dynamics within the quartet. But it would be wrong to think either that a blossoming career would guarantee the cohesion of the group, or that a dragging career would necessarily jeopardise it.

Friendship matters deeply to Krzysztof Chorzelski, viola player of the Belcea Quartet. In a letter to me, he wrote:

I am writing these words during the first days of rehearsals after more than three months of a sudden separation from my quartet friends. Our 'Beethoven season' was interrupted by the coronavirus pandemic, and the resulting lockdown of our respective countries meant that all our concerts got cancelled. From the greatest heights of musical fulfilment, we practically overnight landed in a state of limbo, unsure to this day of what this will mean for our life as a quartet in the long run.

Both the separation and, now, our return to each other have inspired in me many thoughts about the nature of what binds us together.

The first bars we played when we reunited a couple of days ago were the opening of the surreal Scherzo from Beethoven's quartet in C sharp minor, op. 131. What makes playing them together feel so right for me? Surely, the answer lies in more than just the obvious fact of being finely attuned to each other after years of rehearsing and performing together.

The silence of the last three months distilled in my mind what role the quartet that I have been part of for almost a quarter of a century plays in my life. Being an only child, and having grown up surrounded mostly by adults, I missed out on what I consider to be one of life's essential experiences: the carefree companionship of a partner-in-crime, someone my age to go through childhood's adventures with, someone to fight with and, finally, someone who would, perhaps, share the spotlight of my parents' attention and the responsibility that comes with it.

It is one of my life's greatest strokes of luck that in my adulthood, through music, I found the siblings I missed as a child.

While the affectionate bond between us is, no doubt, mutual, my quartet siblings come from much larger families and I am not sure if our musical team has a similar meaning to them. In fact, I believe that some of our past misunderstandings may have come from the unintended burden of expectation I have sometimes put on them.

The sudden lockdown we found ourselves in shifted our focus away from quartet life, but when a few days ago we sat down to play our beloved Beethoven quartets again we were back in the enchanted realm that we share, where the outside world's rules don't apply and where we feel the exhilarating joy of sharing in the mischief of playing together.

WHO OWNS WHAT

———

Income is divided by four: that seems to be a reasonable consensus for a quartet. But where does actual income start? Which costs are quartet costs, and which are personal? Does everyone have to stay in the same hotel? One of the members would be happy with a more modest hotel, because he doesn't care about anything as long as there is a bed. But another thinks that, especially during a tour, comfort matters. How is the extra ticket for the cello settled? Is it a quartet affair or is the cellist alone responsible? He's the one who plays it, after all. The question might seem strange, but it's not a ridiculous one.

Who is treasurer while they are travelling? Should it be the most parsimonious, the one who protects his colleagues from unnecessary expenditure, but ends up giving one or another of them a hard time? Or should it be the generous one, the one who risks being charged with mindless extravagance if, in the name of comfort, he orders three taxis to have a less cramped ride? Is it even necessary to have a treasurer?

Even if they share out all the income, and as a result do not build up any joint property, there will, nonetheless, be property specific to the quartet. In the first place, obviously, there is the name, which is their shared capital and which, as it gets more well known, has a great influence on the level of the fees. But there are also things like, for example, the trophies that come with any awards. And who owns the music library, accumulated over the years? Does everyone own their own parts?

Can anyone, as an individual, claim the quartet's name? What if the person who gave his name to the quartet leaves, possibly intending to found a new quartet – again under his own name – while those who are 'left behind' want to continue what they've begun? Does he who carries the name as a person have the right to give it to another quartet, and deprive his former colleagues of their own history?

Here is a letter I received from Ulrike Petersen, the eponymous founding member and first violinist of the Petersen Quartet:

With interest and admiration, I looked at the home page of the Petersen Quartet today. May I please ask you a question: why is it that the twelve years that connected my own life with the Petersen Quartet have more or less disappeared? And why is it still the 'Petersen Quartet'?

I don't want to pick a petty fight, I just don't understand why the first twelve years should remain hanging there anonymously, particularly as it was such a tough decision for me. I left the quartet in December 1991, and in January my third child was born. The overwhelming reason for my leaving the quartet was that the conflicts between children, quartet and my general family situation became irreconcilable.

I still regard playing string quartets as the ideal way of making music, only now there are other tasks in life for me. Apart from anything else, I have become a mother for a fourth time, so leaving the quartet was certainly the right decision to make.

Ulrike Petersen wrote this to me in September 2003. In March 2007, she rejoined the quartet, playing first violin, alternating with Conrad Muck, who had stepped in for her sixteen years before. Today, the Petersen Quartet no longer exists. Quartet tales.

A BALANCING ACT

In the beginning, they have no obligations, they discuss everything, share everything, even hotel rooms, like brothers and sisters. The quartet – and nothing else – is the centre of their lives. If a quartet member starts a relationship, it means that someone else muscles into the quartet – albeit indirectly. An expanding family can topple the priorities of the quartet, which so far may have been taken for granted. A quartet is an obligation, not only towards a cause but also towards the three other people, and so it's possible that it becomes direct competition for any private relationship. Once a member's partner perceives the quartet as a rival in their relationship, that member finds himself in a zone of enormous tension.

Music is not only about mastering parts, about manual dexterity or ensemble. It's also about inspiration, which makes the difference between a mechanical reproduction and a living performance. Inspiration needs openness. If someone is affected by something that makes him close up against the group, the entire balance can topple. A string quartet happens in real life, and with every day that passes everyone's individual lives change. The collective – for better or for worse – must follow. It must develop accordingly, and must go along with each change in each individual's life. Falling in love, romantic problems, giving birth, the death of a relative, strong emotions in general, concern everyone. In situations such as these, playing together can be affected. It's only mutual respect that makes it possible that each one is allowed to follow his or her own journey of the soul without affecting their unity in the music. Although the connection between the individual members can be quite intense and is always vulnerable to conflicts, the quartet – unlike a marriage – does not demand exclusivity, either emotionally or artistically. It demands nothing but priority.

A successful career means more concerts and more travelling, with a corresponding increase in organising and coordinating. This means the quartet takes on more and more, at least in terms of time. As a result, a certain rationalisation in the relationships becomes necessary. This is the moment when members of a string quartet might begin to call each other colleagues, intuitively drawing a line. Some quartets might go on to make a veritable cult of their need for distance. Finding the balance between emotional intimacy and collegial distance, and readjusting this balance again and again, is part of the core business of a string quartet. Some quartets need a good deal of talking – they discuss everything, and they discuss it to death – while others prefer a resounding silence, waiting for apparently insoluble conflicts to resolve by themselves, in the knowledge that there is no alternative to the quartet for any of them.

This is the most important difference between string quartets and other 'teams'. There are many examples of small working groups that have to function with extreme precision – sports teams, teams of astronauts or those surrounding surgeons. Quite a few of these stay together for years in the same formation. But hardly any other team has the structural equality of a string quartet – or the autonomy. A string quartet has no boss interfering from outside; it's not accountable to any company or any institution – it is accountable to nobody but itself. This means that whatever responsibility there is lies within the group itself. Moreover, no other team demands – as the string quartet does – a lifetime commitment, one that basically affects an entire professional life, and which, therefore, in terms of time, is not unlike a marriage.

We function like a circus, or rather like a theatre company of the sort that works without a director [says Raphaël Merlin]. *As in a cooperative, the responsibility for the production is shared between the members; and it is this lack of hierarchy and of a dominant voice that makes the whole enterprise exhilarating as well as risky. In the orchestral world, one recognises bad conductors by how they always feel the need to interrupt the orchestra without having anything important to contribute. Stopping the musical momentum can simply be a source of exhaustion and exasperation. In a quartet, however, you have to come to an agreement, and the one who interrupts the group, who is guilty of disturbing the common inspiration, triggers a process of reflection that is essential but paradoxical. The one who talks kills the music, but the one who prefers to play instead kills the discussion. No one is without guilt in this game (but everyone is forgivable, and forgiving is a necessary path and frequently pursued!). Even if someone is blameless, he will be blamed for that, too. The one who is overzealous about setting musical decisions in stone digs a grave for matters such as natural phrasing and organic timing. The one who always wants breaks and wants to keep weekends free becomes the dilettante who jeopardises the quality of the group, and the one who perseveres in asking for more rehearsals becomes the workaholic who confuses the means for the end. The one who harps on about stylistic rules because he aspires to rise to the standards of Leopold Mozart's* Gründliche Violinschule *might stifle the creativity of the collective playing, which is a hybrid, the fruit of all the diverse artistic influences that have emerged since Leopold Mozart. And the one who chooses to ignore developments*

in 'historically informed' interpretation will be the dinosaur who blocks
a full view of the works. The one who advocates for contemporary
creation at all costs, even when the composition in question has no
future, can be a snob betraying his own aesthetic principles, while the
defender of neoclassicism and crossover becomes the reactionary of the
group, the opportunistic populiser. In short, all possible contrasts and
contradictions are crystallised in the quartet; it's the distillate of
everything that raises questions. It is a four-sided mirror, a citizens'
forum, a mobile mini-stage that never rests on its laurels. It is the
impossible quest for an indefinable ideal.

What Raphaël Merlin does not mention here is that the public is part of any performing artist's life. It looms large, too, inside the social microcosm that is the string quartet. Just by performing, its members get confronted with themselves, and many a necessary internal discussion is triggered from the outside. This kind of help can be completely accidental: an intelligent review, a recording of a concert, a simple technical question from a listener or a comment from a friend. The public cannot necessarily protect a quartet from a crisis, but it might help detect a smouldering conflict before it ignites.

HOOKED BY THE MUSIC

'Because the music caught us, never let us go, because
we have found a home in this kind of music making.'
– Pacifica Quartet

There are notions that make you prick up your ears: a 'home' signifies something familiar, intimate, stable and enveloping. Everyone knows that it's not always peaceful at home, but this is the place from which you leave and to which you return. Clearly, the Pacifica Quartet understands the string quartet as a way of life – beyond music itself. In a world where individualism is a cult and singularity prevails, the string quartet can serve as an example of working and living together. That's how I understand and interpret the biographies of two famous exemplary quartets of the past century: the Amadeus Quartet and the LaSalle Quartet.

Three members of the LaSalle Quartet originated from Germany. Two of them, Walter Levin and Peter Kamnitzer, had emigrated just in time. Henry Meyer survived Auschwitz and went to America only after the war, and after having lived in Paris for some time. The two longest-serving cellists of the quartet, Jack Kirstein, and later on Lee Fiser, were both born in America.

The three Viennese members of the Amadeus Quartet, Norbert

Brainin, Siegmund Nissel and Peter Schidlof, did not meet in Vienna. All three of them were born in the Austrian capital in the early twenties and had come to England in 1939 as refugees, two of them through a Kindertransport. It was only in 1940 that they met in an internment camp for so-called 'friendly enemy aliens' on the Isle of Man – through the music that was an important part of life at the camp. After being released in 1941, all three became pupils of Max Rostal, who had taught at the Berlin conservatoire before having to emigrate to England himself in 1934. That was how they met their British number four, Martin Lovett, the future cellist of the quartet – his then-girlfriend (later his wife) studied with Max Rostal too. Muriel Nissel, the wife of Siegmund, the second violinist, captured the moving success story of the Amadeus Quartet in a lovely book, *Married to the Amadeus.*

Both quartets were formed at around the same time, and they were active on the international stage for about the same amount of time – the Amadeus from 1948 to 1987, and the LaSalle from 1946 to 1987. As different as they were in musical terms, they were similar in the fortunes that brought their members together. Emigrés in a foreign land, they found a kind of home within their quartets. In both cases, LaSalle and Amadeus, German was the language of the quartet. The indigenous cellists for each had to learn German upon joining, both mastering it perfectly as time went on.

'The joint work on the music,' said Günter Pichler of the Alban Berg Quartett, 'demands an unconditional "opening up". You can't pretend at this high level of communication. If it works out, it's ideal.' This ambitious way of communicating requires the participants to engage in a personal relationship with each other as well, to find and develop a language of their own for their joint music-making. A joint interpretation starts when a verbal agreement isn't necessary any more, where language ends – in a kind of nakedness, free of courtesies, shyness, consideration, formality, Schadenfreude or vanity. String quartet music is played on the seam that connects the individual with the collective. Here, it's not merely the consolidation of individual interpretations: it's about a joint interpretation, in the development of which all four are involved, together with their individual characteristics. Merging like this on an intellectual, artistic and emotional level is dependent on a multitude of factors. The members must focus on the cause (the quartet as the fulfilment of the artistic and professional aims of the individuals), and they must agree on the necessity (the quartet as their livelihood) as well as on the inevitable (success as their motivation). Daily rehearsing means extreme closeness and interdependence on each other; travelling together, sharing public appearances and having success together means intimacy. In this shared space, music is just one of the many areas around which the four have to shape their community.

This is how Oliver Wille, violinist of the Kuss Quartet, defines his interest in the string quartet as a way of life:

Probably, it's curiosity that makes me play in a string quartet in the first place. Curiosity about creativity and about the artistic challenge. It is this kind of thing that makes you take on the hardships of conflict and uncertainty, and the lack of comfort or a steady life. And eventually, you do find your reward in moments of joy, harmony and uniqueness, when you know you have experienced something special.

In a string quartet, you're dealing on a daily basis with a genre that seems to be the epitome of bourgeoisie and conservatism, only it isn't necessarily like that. There have been textbooks written about the quartet as a modern genre, and it's true: this rigid structure of four players can be so incredibly mobile – flexible in every possible direction.

This is what I'm interested in at the moment: how does an ensemble of this kind fit into today's world of music – into our society, even –

without giving up its identity and its artistic ambition? On the one hand, you deal with the great works, as they are called, the milestones of the art of the string quartet. And then there are the newer compositions that have to carry the weight of the old ones – yet they still have something in common. Both seem to be less bourgeois the more progressive they are in musical terms, and they interact with each other. So, is there no outdated element of petit-bourgeoisie in chamber music after all? As a string quartet, should you perform in those venerable, fascinating and important concert series – some of which are amazingly old – or should you prefer the cool metropolitan club scene to get younger listeners engaged? Is it appropriate to condescend to experienced listeners by playing snippets and giving explanations? Is this kind of help imperative for a young audience? Do you follow traditional ideas of programming, or do you sometimes present familiar works in unexpected settings? Do you combine string quartets with other arts – for example, the theatre – and do you work to create conceptual programmes?

There are no rules, no directors, and actually no famous 'footsteps' in which to follow.

Love of experimentation, involvement with art – while hopefully managing to keep the concept of art as indefinite as possible – can be an adventure. The charm lies, I think, in the individual voice for which you alone are responsible, which has to fit into the organism of the quartet, which helps to shape the character of the music. Out of this, the spirit of adventure is conjured. It is often said that quartet compositions are 'a composer's field of experimentation', and composers do quite often take amazing risks in the writing of those voices. Unlike piano compositions of the same artistic ambition, the score consists of four lines. Is this why each voice – and each person in the ensemble – receives special attention?

At any rate, you feel permanently challenged, observed, found out. Whether it's in Haydn or in the German avant-garde composer Helmut Lachenmann – you always have the feeling that the studying will never end...

One more reason why string quartet playing can become addictive: who could ever claim to have played one of these works in an entirely satisfying way? Whether you feel bad about it or not, it seems that the vital search for an appropriate coherence and for the author's truth is never ending.

This is how Ori Kam, from the Jerusalem Quartet, describes his fascination with the string quartet as a genre:

The quartet repertoire is an immense canon of masterpieces. So much so that many eminent quartets never consider lesser-known or rarely-played composers. Almost every great composer wrote string quartets, and often these compositions are among their best work. Approaching a masterpiece with a rich history of memorable performances is quite different from performing an obscure piece or a new commission. Masterpieces require a strange cocktail of humility and self-determination: humility towards the text and tradition, and the self-determination to meet both of these at eye-level.

I grew up listening to the great quartets, both live and recorded. One thing that always struck me, is that while each quartet achieves a unique effect, the musical choices they make are almost identical. By this I mean that the tempos they pick, the places where they slow down, climax, phrase, or use portamento, are almost exactly the same. This is probably because, in most cases, the music itself is so meticulously notated. If this is so, the question is, where do they inject their own personality or ego? In my opinion, it is primarily in the sound. When a phone is answered, it's primarily the voice at the other end, not the words said or how they are said, that allows us to recognise the speaker. This is also true with musicians, particularly string players.

At its core, music is generosity. First and foremost, between the musicians and their listeners. In our day-to-day life, we are very careful about touching others, yet in the concert hall we caress, jab and even slap hundreds of people. Through the touch of our sound, which is perhaps the most fundamental physical human experience, we share the deepest and most ethereal places in our soul. We also share a generous relationship with the composers. They give us the vehicle to share our deepest truths, and we give them immortality. Finally, in my experience, playing in a string quartet is also an exercise in generosity. Knowing when to take the spotlight, and when to help make others shine. When to join and when to resist. Playing as a member of a string quartet is a never-ending challenge to become a better human being every day: more self-aware, more generous, more considerate, more social, and more present and connected to the people and world around us. I consider it a privilege, and could not imagine a better life.

UNIQUENESS

Intermission chats, green room conversations:

'That Schubert was divine, absolutely peerless!'

'They played the Berg so wonderfully today – it should never be played any other way.'

'In the Bartók you could really hear who they are; not a heartstring left untugged.'

'For their opus 135, I'd follow them anywhere.'

'Ligeti – a revelation. I thought he was completely inaccessible, but they play it as if it was a Haydn *divertimento*. Such a sense of humour!'

How do you reconcile these declarations of uniqueness with the accusation that you often hear: that everyone always plays the same? If you ask the musicians, their complaint is the other way around. The audience always wants to hear the same repertoire! Performing works that are played by others too is part of being a classical musician. It's true that the source they draw upon – in this case, the string quartet literature – is practically inexhaustible. But those who strive for an international classical career will be measured by their performances of the great classics. That's where the fiercest competition plays out.

Just as actors want to become known for their Hamlet or their Juliet, quartet musicians have the vision that the name of their quartet would go down in history linked with some of the legendary titles – 'Death and the Maiden', 'Intimate Letters', 'Métamorphoses Nocturnes', 'Emperor', 'From My Life', 'Lyric Suite', 'Cavatina', *Heiliger Dankgesang eines Genesenden*', '*Muss es sein?*' – or mysterious figures, like 'Brahms 67', 'Mozart 387', 'Haydn 76/5', 'Bartók 5'.[9]

In an interview I conducted with Walter Levin in Basle in January 2006, he told me:

In Bartók's third string quartet, there is a place where the two violins suddenly have to play way up the G string. What do quartets do? Virtually every time they get there, they cheat!

They don't play it on the G string. It's dead easy to play if you play it on the D string instead, in third position, and for the normal listener – so they say – it doesn't make a difference anyway. Wouldn't it be more important to play it in tune than to have this slight difference of timbre? Well, why did Bartók put it there? Precisely because of the risk!

That particular element of tension, when you throw yourself off a high ski jump, is just something completely different if you only jump from half a metre while pretending that you came from much higher up. It looks completely different.

9 'Death and the Maiden': String Quartet in D minor, D 810, by Franz Schubert; 'Intimate Letters': String Quartet no. 2 by Leoš Janáček; *Métamorphoses Nocturnes*': String Quartet no. 1 by György Ligeti; 'Emperor': String Quartet op. 76/3 by Joseph Haydn; 'From my Life': String Quartet no. 1 by Bedřich Smetana; 'Lyric Suite': String Quartet by Alban Berg; 'Cavatina': fifth movement from String Quartet op.130 by Ludwig van Beethoven; *Heiliger Dankgesang eines Genesenden* (Holy Thanksgiving Song of a Convalescent)': third movement from String Quartet op. 132 by Ludwig van Beethoven; '*Muss es sein?* (Must it be?)': from the fourth movement of String Quartet op. 135 by Ludwig van Beethoven; 'Brahms 67': String Quartet no. 3, op. 67 by Johannes Brahms; 'Mozart 387': String Quartet no. 14, K 387 by Wolfgang Amadeus Mozart; 'Haydn 76/5': String Quartet op. 76 no. 5, nicknamed in German *Friedhofsquartett* (Graveyard Quartet) because the second movement is often played at funerals, and because it contains so many *Kreuze* (sharps – the same word as 'crosses' in German).

It's not only about playing something perfectly, it's also about all the other components that are involved, even if an outsider can't hear them. I can! If I listen to a quartet playing this bit, I can tell blindfolded whether they tried to play it up the G string or if they made things easier for themselves. Another popular thing to do is changing what's written. It's easier regrouping a chord from what was written by the composer. But when you redistribute the notes of a chord, you change its sound.

What does it mean, playing on the G string in this place? First of all, it means playing what the composer, in this case, Bartók, prescribes. That's the way he wants it. Sure, it's difficult. It's about more than just the pitch, it's about a timbre, and quite often also about a distortion, which can be part of that. Demanding these qualities of articulation implies that there have to be so-called 'ugly' sounds as well, which you have to play in an ugly way, and that you don't sacrifice everything to a supposedly beautiful sound. It has to sound true, and it has to be true to what was intended. Very often, that's quite far from a beautiful sound.

There are many types of sound production that have absolutely nothing to do with the primitive idea of what's beautiful. Apart from this, the concept of what is 'beautiful' varies – beauty is in the eye of the beholder, after all. Thank God that we don't all find the same things beautiful. What's beautiful for one is hideous for another! Something that is generally considered acceptable or even desirable nowadays, might have been thought unacceptable or even completely impossible at other times.

Mastering a score – in terms of reading it, playing the right notes, conquering the complicated rhythms – is not enough on its own. It's about leaving recognisable tracks. A strong statement requires a deep inner resonance rooted in tradition and culture, in a language – both in the musical and in the linguistic sense – and in a history, which is a personal, but not only a personal one.

Günter Pichler says:

The four members of a quartet should come from the same cultural and social background and should, ideally, have the same kind of education. With us, we had all read the same books – and if we hadn't, there was the advice that we should. So, the education should obviously be on the same level. Because if one says, 'I've seen the composer's manuscript and that's why I think that those wedges in this Mozart here should really be taken seriously, because they don't look like dots or dashes, so the editor pencilled in wedges there,' everyone has to try and be on this same level of knowledge. There are differences everywhere, but as long as the one who doesn't read picks up what the others have read, or if he gets it from somewhere else in conversation, then everything's fine.

Quartets that gather their members from different continents have a more difficult time of it. They must build a lot of bridges to overcome the lack of common ground – differences in language, in ideas of rhythm and time, and in basic educational principles and other traditions. For these quartets, being part of a distinctive music 'school' or having a teacher can help them piece together a repertoire.

If Hungarian musicians play Hungarian music, or if French players interpret French composers, people like to think that their performances are authentic. They may well be 'authentic', but on the other hand, this is just one possible way of performing. Having a work interpreted by musicians who are foreigners in terms of tradition or language can be equally gripping and touching. It is bathed in a different light, conceived under different principles.

When the LaSalle Quartet wanted to put Ravel's String Quartet in F major on the programme of their Paris concert in 1954, it was allowed only after a bitter struggle. The organiser suspected it would be considered outragous for an American quartet to perform a French work in Paris. The audience, however, reacted enthusiastically, and the day after the concert, a newspaper published a review brimming over with praise. One had never heard the work played better, but that was hardly surprising, as only French musicians could grasp its spirit. With razor-sharp reasoning, the reviewer had inferred the national origin of the quartet from its name, LaSalle.

The Alban Berg Quartett probably didn't find it difficult to declare their allegiance to the composers of Vienna – which obviously included the German composers Beethoven and Brahms – or to prioritise the relationship with Vienna in their choice of works. Haydn, Mozart, Beethoven, Schubert and Brahms, and the so-called Second Viennese School, with Schönberg, Webern and Berg, along with contemporaneous composers like Haubenstock-Ramati or Urbanner, and also composers who stayed and wrote music in Vienna, like Dvořák, Lutosławski and Berio – these are all associated with the name of 'Vienna'. (Actually, there is hardly any composer of distinction who didn't spend at least some time in Vienna.) That's why the repertoire list of the Alban Berg Quartett (see pages 106–107) was a very Viennese affair, and, incidentally, also a comprehensive list of the milestones of string quartet literature up to the middle of the twentieth century.

A repertoire doesn't emerge out of thin air. It's the quartet's very own distillation of internal and external principles, compromises, coincidences, encounters with scores, with other musicians and with composers – encounters that may excite curiosity or open doors. It's the musical biography of a quartet. Every single work has at least one story attached to it. Some of these are funny, others recall grievous pain, and most of them are never told. Like a quartet's name and its sound – which is difficult to describe in words – its repertoire is an identifying mark that is inseparable from the quartet itself. It tells you what manner of musical spirit the quartet is, or has become.

The expressive capacity of a quartet is utterly reliant on a consensus regarding the choice and interpretation of each individual work. For example, the violist might have always wanted to play 'From my Life' by Smetana, an extremely emotional, romantic work that has big viola solos. The second violinist, who feels diffident about any romanticism (he is always a bit worried that it might slip into kitsch), might prefer instead to engage with Schönberg's third string quartet, a somewhat unwieldy and ostensibly arid work, which is an intellectual as well as a musical challenge. Given that the other two members of the quartet are happy with either piece, a productive compromise could be to include both in the programme. This would, first of all, require the two with the individual wishes to open up to each other's preferences, so each could expect from the other that his 'own' piece is taken seriously. In addition, each one of them could take responsibility and a leading role with respect to his desired piece. He would need to explain what it is about it that touches him, and to convince the one who had been resisting it to love it to a certain extent.

If a soloist feels that a piece doesn't really suit him, he doesn't have to explain or justify his discomfort. He can simply decide whether to include it in his repertoire or to drop it. In a string quartet, things are, by definition, a bit more complicated: all four members have to be able to identify with each work they choose, and all four must want to play it. How do you discuss – in a group of four – matters of taste, musical affinity and emotional attachment? What happens if one of the four really loves a particular work, but he is the only one who does? Or if someone argues against a work just as passionately as someone else

REPERTOIRE OF THE
ALBAN BERG QUARTETT

JOHANN SEBASTIAN BACH

Art of the Fugue

ZBIGNIEW BARGIELSKI

String Quartet no. 4,
'Le temps ardent'

BÉLA BARTÓK

String Quartet op. 7 no. 1
String Quartet op. 17 no. 2
String Quartet no. 3
String Quartet no. 4
String Quartet no. 5
String Quartet no. 6

LUDWIG VAN BEETHOVEN

String Quartet op. 18/1
String Quartet op. 18/2
String Quartet op. 18/3
String Quartet op. 18/4
String Quartet op. 18/5
String Quartet op. 18/6
String Quartet op. 59/1
String Quartet op. 59/2
String Quartet op. 59/3
String Quartet op. 74
String Quartet op. 95
String Quartet op. 127
String Quartet op. 130/133
String Quartet op. 131
String Quartet op. 132
String Quartet op. 135

ALBAN BERG

String Quartet op. 3
Lyric Suite for String Quartet

LUCIANO BERIO

Notturno

JOHANNES BRAHMS

Piano Quintet F minor op. 34
String Quartet C minor op. 51/1
String Quartet A minor op. 51/2
String Quartet B flat
major op. 67
Clarinet Quintet op. 115
String Quintet op. 111

BENJAMIN BRITTEN

String Quartet no. 3

CLAUDE DEBUSSY

String Quartet G minor

ANTONÍN DVOŘÁK

String Quartet op. 51
Piano Quintet op. 81
String Quartet op. 105

ROMAN HAUBENSTOCK-RAMATI

String Quartet no. 2

JOSEPH HAYDN

String Quartet op. 33/3
String Quartet op. 74/3
String Quartet op. 76/1
String Quartet op. 76/2
String Quartet op. 76/3
String Quartet op. 76/4
String Quartet op. 76/5
String Quartet op. 76/6
String Quartet op. 77/1
String Quartet op. 77/2

LEOŠ JANÁČEK
String Quartet no. 1,
'Kreutzer Sonata'
String Quartet no. 2
'Intimate Letters'

GYÖRGY KURTÀG
12 Microludes for
String Quartet op. 13

WITOLD LUTOSŁAWSKI
String Quartet (1964)

FELIX MENDELSSOHN-
BARTHOLDY
String Quartet op. 12
String Quartet op. 13

WOLFGANG AMADEUS MOZART
String Quartet K 387
Piano Quintet K 414
String Quartet K 421
String Quartet K 428
String Quartet K 458
String Quartet K 464
String Quartet K 465
Piano Quartet K 493
String Quartet K 499
String Quartet K 575
String Quartet K 589
String Quartet K 590

MAURICE RAVEL
String Quartet F major

WOLFGANG RIHM
String Quartet no. 4

ALFRED SCHNITTKE
4th String Quartet

ARNOLD SCHÖNBERG
String Quartet op. 30 no. 3
String Trio op. 45

FRANZ SCHUBERT
String Quartet D 87
String Quartet D 173
String Quartet D 703 'Quartett-Satz'
String Quartet D 804 'Rosamunde'
String Quartet D 810
'Death and the Maiden'
String Quartet D 887
String Quintet C major D 956
Piano Quintet in A major D. 667
'Trout Quintet'

ROBERT SCHUMANN
String Quartet A major op. 41 no. 3

DMITRI SHOSTAKOVICH
String Quartet op. 108 no. 7

JOHANN STRAUSS (FATHER)
Piano Quintet E flat major op. 44
Waltz/Polka/Dances

ERICH URBANNER
String Quartet no. 4

ANTON VON WEBERN
5 Movements for String Quartet op. 5
6 Bagatelles for String Quartet op. 9
String Quartet op. 28

HUGO WOLF
Italian Serenade for String Quartet

argues in favour of it? How does one player feel if the three others pressurise him to play a work he doesn't feel comfortable with, and he can't keep his mind from wandering when he is practising it? You don't have to be a musician to be able to imagine the tension and loneliness you might feel if no one shares your passions.

Arnold Steinhardt describes how the Guarneri Quartet met every autumn for a 'reading session' during which they would choose their repertoire for the following season. Each of them would bring the music he had always wanted to play, and everything would be played through. Year after year, when it was his turn, John Dalley, the second violinist, would put the music of Sibelius' 'Voces intimae' ('Intimate Voices') on their stands – a perennial running gag within the quartet. John Dalley and David Soyer, the cellist, both loved that work, while Arnold Steinhardt and the violist, Michael Tree, both disliked it. According to their highly developed democratic tradition, it was part of the game to treat every request equally, and so, each year, they played through the piece. Arnold Steinhardt recalls a particular day when they were playing it for the umpteenth time:

> *This time, I found myself touched by the opening, and swept along by the music's agitation. That momentum, once established, carried me through all five movements. The part of me that had disliked this work lost substance and then, like any respectable ghost, disappeared into thin air. I loved the Sibelius, and as if that wasn't enough of a surprise, Michael also had changed his mind. In the course of twenty-five minutes, all four of us unexpectedly found our opinions realigned and unanimous.*

The process of deciding what pieces to include in a quartet's repertoire is always difficult – even if it ends up successful. Walter Levin talked about this in our interview:

If a quartet wants to leave its mark, it must clearly define its position with regard to its repertoire, its way of playing, and its style of presenting itself. It really has to turn itself into an identifiable unit in order to make a difference between itself and everyone else.

How do you do this? How do you develop a specific musical interest, a specific direction?

By immersing yourself in lots of music, by listening to lots of music. And if you're in a group of four, all four of you have to do this. I had big problems with some pieces in my own quartet, because no one wanted to play them – they were difficult, or they came across as romantic 'secondary music'. Sometimes it was said: 'This piece has been around for such a long time, and no one has ever played it, there must be a reason. We don't know what reason, but basically, it can't be that good.' That's a misconception. You have to be able to form your own opinion. You have to learn to recognise the quality of a piece by yourself, by means of the score.

What are the criteria by which you judge a score or a piece? That's a very difficult question. By what criteria do you judge music? How do you pick a piece? I once presented a somewhat cynical ten-point plan that addressed this question, during a lecture in Cincinnati:

Ten Commandments:

1 *If it's nice: avoid it.*
2 *If the critics trash it: have a look at it.*
3 *If the critics praise it: better steer clear.*
4 *If it's written in a new notation system: try transcribing it into a conventional system – and if it works, forget it.*
5 *If it's naïve – let it be.*
6 *If it's very naïve, have a closer look – maybe you missed the point.*
7 *If it seems complex, make sure that it's not just hard to play.*

8 *If it strikes a familiar chord or resonates in a pleasant way,
recommend it to a music-lover.*

9 *If it fulfils your innermost wishes, drop it; a good work needs you
to create the very wish it will fulfil.*

10 *If it sounds like a string quartet, it's not necessarily bad, but
probably is.*

*Emptiness is fashionable again these days. It's exactly what's in
demand. Things are supposed to be simple and not that intellectual, not
that complicated. But why not? Aren't we supposed to exercise our
brains any more? Does everything have to be a kind of easy listening?
Contemporary music suffers from this.*

*My choices were never convenient. But, again and again, it would turn
out that a choice I had made was a good one – we would make a
recording of it that would be spectacularly successful – and they began to
trust me. I got so much resistance over Zemlinsky's second string quartet!*

*We'd already played Zemlinsky no. 3. It hadn't been too hard to
persuade them to do that. It wasn't that long, and it wasn't that difficult
to play – it was somehow manageable. And then, when Stravinsky came
along, saying: 'What, Zemlinsky? He's the greatest conductor I ever heard
in my entire life', Zemlinsky suddenly became a big thing! And here was
I, suggesting Zemlinsky no. 2: a gigantic work, difficult, very long. 'Come
on, do we really have to? Let's not, no one wants to hear that stuff any
more.' Wrong! It turned into one of our biggest successes! Bestseller for
Deutsche Grammophon in America. Things like that convinced my
colleagues that I have an eye.*

*We learned the pieces because we thought they were interesting. That's
it! One has to be caught by the piece and the music in the first place.
And then you can see whether something comes out of it. Sometimes it
would take years for someone to take a particular work from us. We*

offered Zemlinsky no. 3 in Europe on our first tour after learning it. It
was only picked once – by Südwestfunk Baden-Baden, for a radio
recording. An excellent recording, by the way, I still like to listen to it.
Zemlinsky's music hadn't made it here yet, and when I came up with his
second string quartet, my colleagues said: 'Why should we bother
learning another one if it's just going to sit in the drawer again?' A few
years later, we couldn't play enough Zemlinsky. If it's about getting good
pieces established, you sometimes have to have a little patience ...

I did need a majority for a piece to be played. I couldn't simply decree:
'This piece is going to be played!' Instead, I had to get at least two of
the others on my side. It's no use just being authoritarian, because the
others won't be up for it. I convinced them, one by one. I learned that
you're more successful at convincing people if you get them by
themselves, if you deal with them individually, if you make your case
and take your time. You need to have proved that the suggestions you're
making aren't completely arbitrary, that they aren't just for the hell of it,
but that they represent a direction. (In the beginning, for example,
Henry [the second violinist of the LaSalle Quartet] *had never played*
a Bartók quartet; he thought it was hideous!) They mostly ended up
agreeing, sometimes maybe a bit reluctantly, but I never dictated.

REHEARSING

The way a quartet rehearses, how much and at which times of day or night – all this is determined by the quartet itself. String quartets usually set up precise schedules for their working time. They keep regular hours, the number of hours is specified, and, if at all possible, they don't exceed them.

Here is Walter Levin again:

Basically, we rehearsed six days a week and had one day off. When we first started out – actually, for many years – it was four hours a day, and towards the end, three hours a day. After a tour, we used to take a couple of days' break, and in the summer, we would always take our holidays. After five or six weeks off, we would meet, for example in Flims in the Swiss Alps, to study the pieces for the upcoming season. That would still be a sort of semi-holiday. Over about five weeks or so, we'd rehearse in the morning in the ski school – because we'd all be living in separate places – and in the afternoons and evenings, everyone would be free. Everything was already prepared before the summer break. There was a precise timetable for which pieces were worked on, and when, which gave everyone the possibility, and the obligation, of preparing their part in advance. We figured things out in detail: for one

---

particular piece, we'll need about a week, so we'll keep two thirds of the rehearsal time for this piece, and one third for a second piece, as that one is easier. We'll need two hours for the Zemlinsky, and one hour for a new classical piece. Like this for one week. And if we still need a second week for the Zemlinsky, we could include another, easier piece, which we had pencilled in for later. So that, by the end of those five weeks, we would have worked through everything we needed for the new season. Which would include refreshing pieces from earlier seasons that we'd decided to revive for the new season's repertoire.

A preparation period like this would happen once à year, and the other rehearsals were our normal ones for concerts and tours as they came up. For those, we rehearsed on a daily basis, to a meticulous schedule that laid down how and what we would work on one particular week or the next, so that everyone could practise in advance.

As a precondition for each rehearsal, we had the rule that everyone had to be on top of his own part. Rehearsals are for rehearsing things that have been practised individually. You can't rehearse what hasn't been practised. Rehearsals are not for practising!

If someone, for some reason, hadn't practised his part, I would say: 'Let's forget it for today.' No point rehearsing then. It didn't happen too often, though. On the other hand, sometimes it was the other way round: Lee [Fiser, cellist] normally needed only a half or a third of the time the others needed to learn a new piece. So, he would feel bored. He already had it down pat! This happens, too. If someone is on top of his part already, that's not as bad as if somebody else isn't there yet. Now, if someone isn't on top of his part yet, and refuses to practise: there's a problem. You've got to solve this with individual conversations. Otherwise, things would go wrong, obviously. There would be quite a rumpus, wouldn't there?

You've got to watch out, here. If someone has a weakness in a certain

---

area, for example in the rhythm, and if he makes the same mistake over and over again, he has to work harder on it. If someone just can't manage a specific problem, you sit down with him, one-on-one, to work on it. You've always got to say something like: 'Listen, I need this myself, too! We've got to solve this problem together. We have to click together, find a way somehow, so the entries come smoothly, OK?' Or maybe: '... so the intonation works there.'

One immediately recognises pupils of Walter Levin's by their sheet music: oversized, sometimes pieced together in bizarre ways, never fitting properly on any music stand. These monsters are home-made parts, cobbled together from scores that have been photocopied and enlarged (string quartet scores are printed pocket-size and are not legible from the music stand). Over many hours at the kitchen table, they get cut up and glued together in a way that also makes page turns possible. Some quartets use parts like this only while studying a piece, but play concerts from parts that are printed in the normal size. Others keep the monsters.

Quartets differ in their methods of approaching a new piece for the repertoire. But even within an individual quartet, not all players necessarily agree. One player prefers to listen to the piece before learning it, so he starts by getting himself all the relevant and available recordings. Another has his own way of taking possession of the piece, by reading his part and the score – he listens to other interpretations only after developing his own ideas about the work.

A quartet rehearses a composition by the (not too well-known) Spanish composer Juan Crisóstomo de Arriaga for the first time. The violinist speaks with great enthusiasm about a recording which he has bought, and which he thinks is phenomenal. The cellist stares at him, aghast: he, too, has listened to this recording, along with two other ones, and it's exactly this recording that he thinks is stilted and a long way away from the ideal he aspires to for his own quartet.

How do you discuss, how do you negotiate with each other, when everything is about breathing and emotions? How loud is loud, and what counts as quiet? A tempo that is metronomically fixed can seem – depending on the individual player's way of breathing or phrasing – faster when it's played by one player than by another. A new piece for the repertoire almost certainly results in passionate arguments. Volker Jacobsen, violist of the Artemis Quartett at the time, explained to me the process of learning a new work.

There are three wash cycles. The first cycle is the transition from individual practising to rehearsing – from the single part to the ensemble. You read together, play together, and don't criticise very much. (Valentin Erben, cellist of the Alban Berg Quartett, used to say: 'Don't criticise me until I can play it!')

The second wash cycle is purely functional, using the metronome, and pencils for bowings and other technical stuff. You need it for organising the ensemble, for the exact adjustment of the voices in relation to each other. Already at this stage, vigorous discussions can emerge, but they are based on factual questions (in the score of publisher X, it's written in a different way, in the recording of Y Quartet, the tempo of this movement is quite a lot faster, etc.).

The third wash cycle is awful, because now it's about making the work your own – that is, the quartet's own – working it out and interpreting it. Now the struggle begins: who gives way when, who accepts, who decides? Comments can be embellished with destructive accusations regarding the abilities of your colleagues, and can result in lots of tears and curses. The pressure of an approaching performance only increases the vehemence of the arguments. This cycle is the spin cycle!

Wash cycles! Players in other quartets react in very different ways to this metaphor. Some are delighted, others are shocked. How do you reach an agreement if you don't feel the same way? Who can be right in such a situation? When is it insight, when is it resignation? How can a musician be passionate and at the same time have his emotions constrained? When, after a period of ten years or so, the Alban Berg Quartett put Schubert's String Quartet D 87 on its programme once again, cellist Valentin Erben picked up his part and found a note that he must have written during the rehearsals ten years before: 'I'm going to quit giving up, right now.'

'It feels right.' This is how musicians describe – in a precise and at the same time vague manner – the kind of kinship quartet players mutually seek in each other. It is tempting to understand this as the players sharing the same intuitions, something which, again, is particularly important with respect to the choice of repertoire. One would hope that a wider scope of affinities results in a more straightforward and less conflict-laden cooperation – also in the sense of what Bernard Fournier had in mind when he spoke about the four instruments merging into a single one. But, on the downside, it poses the risk that the quartet just sounds too monochrome. The more the musicians differ, the greater the chance of assembling a wide and nuanced range of colours, albeit under conditions that are more difficult. So, it's more that the 'rightness' of the feeling indicates an affinity in the common quest. In one quartet, the permanent feud between the two violinists was explained like this: it is irrelevant, because they both want the same thing. The quarrel results from differences about the wording of the message, and not about its core.

Günter Pichler says:

The composer, or the work, keeps hovering above everything. Added to which, there are the rules of interpretation. Rules that obviously have exceptions, and that have to be supplemented with life, and soul and heart. But the basic rules are evident, whether by education or by acquired knowledge. The composer is the authority. And we try, by using certain rules, to achieve an interpretation of this composer.

The rules are there, or the composer wrote them down. In earlier times, they didn't write down very much: there are no indications, no piano, no forte, no nothing. No articulation slurs. Nothing at all. If publishers like Henle or Doblinger or Bärenreiter publish an urtext edition[10] of, say, a Haydn quartet, and this piece doesn't have any articulation slurs or dynamic markings, it doesn't mean you can just play it that way. Instead, you need a huge amount of experience in order to put those details in, or you've got to educate yourself (for example, by reading the relevant books). The downside of an urtext edition is that it doesn't include anything – you, as a player, have to find out, by yourself, the rules that were in place at the time of the composition and that made indications redundant. For this, you've got to learn about the time when the works were created, and you've got to expose yourself to historical performance practice.

Take, for example, Andreas Moser, pupil of Joseph Joachim [a famous violinist of the nineteenth century and friend of Johannes Brahms], and later his teaching assistant and successor: he published, among other things, an edition of the complete Haydn string quartets. He had this experience. Not only was he a brilliant mind, not only had he learned a lot from Joachim – but he was still in direct contact with the tradition [stemming from Haydn].

---

10 Urtext (German for 'original' text) editions try to get as close as possible to what the composer wrote. Older editions, like the famous and widely used edition of the Haydn string quartets by Andreas Moser, usually add quite a large number of technical and interpretative details that are not included in the composer's material. They arise from the editor's expert knowledge and practical experience and thus form part of an interpretation.

Because the rules were less and less observed and so were sinking into oblivion, composers began to establish their own rules. Look at the tempo indications in Beethoven; look at articulation slurs, phrasing slurs. For instance, at some point, Brahms writes a slur across eight bars. You can't execute that in a strict sense; you can't technically play it in one single bow, or, if you're a singer, sing it in one single breath. Instead, it means that it's intended as one line, as a structured phrase. You've got to breathe it in a sensible way, to really perform the complete phrase in a demonstrative way. Differences in metronome markings in Bartók – for example, you find increases, like from fifty-six to fifty-eight beats per minute – can be so minuscule that an average listener or a normal player would hardly be able to perceive them. What these numbers mean is: please be sure not to get slower at this point, instead, up the tempo, get a bit pushy. Over time, these indications in composers' scores became more and more numerous, and you end up with over-indicated parts, like in 'Livre pour Quatuor' by Pierre Boulez, where there's a new tempo for every single bar, and within one single bar three or four different dynamic markings. This was why Boulez initially refused to release the piece. Eventually, we were the first to play excerpts from it. I think Klaus Lauer [the music enthusiast and organiser of the Badenweiler festival] *pushed him to allow it. Before we played to him, I apologised that we weren't able to meet his demands, because there were too many of them, and they were not doable.*

AN ATTEMPT AT BEGINNING TO SET DOWN RULES FOR REHEARSING

––––––

Günter Pichler gave me a wonderful document from his archive. Thomas Kakuska, the late violist of the Alban Berg Quartett – he died in 2005 – had suggested setting up rules for discussions during their rehearsals, and Günter Pichler had made a first attempt. Here it is, dated 26 August 1984.

If a member of the ABQ [Alban Berg Quartett] *criticises another member (in musical or technical terms), the critique should be delivered as specifically and as precisely as possible. For example:'I imagine this place here as more luminous (or as more rhythmical, or more gentle, more elegant, etc.)' or:'Intonation here or bowing technique there is not right.' At the request of the recipient, the critic is allowed – if he can – to elaborate on his critique. Any intervention by a third party is to be avoided if possible.*

If the problem is not fixed by the next rehearsal, the critic should offer his support by giving brief advice. Only after all this should the issue be addressed collectively in the rehearsal.

If it is the general playing together or the general intonation that is not satisfactory in a certain place, a critical comment, including an indication of a focus (intonation, or playing together, or character) is

––––––

permissible, and need not lead to discussion. For example: 'Why don't we all take a closer look at this particular aspect of that bar?'

In my view, one purpose of rehearsals is to allow everyone to figure out what still needs to be worked on individually. For example, where do insecurities appear that didn't happen or that didn't get picked up during individual practice? Confusion can arise because of other voices joining in, because the sound levels need adjusting, because you feel rhythmically constrained, or because the intonation gets unsettled by a precarious combination of intervals. This wouldn't necessarily mean that you haven't worked enough on a certain place, but it could mean, for example, that this place (because of the complicating effect of the ensemble) just needs to be practised into the ground. (In my own case, for example, this happens quite often because, in a rehearsal, in certain places, nervousness can suddenly take over, which reveals problems that didn't emerge during personal practice.) I think, though, that it's an illusion to imagine that daily practice isn't vulnerable to carelessness or negligence. So, any criticism should be gratefully accepted, without giving too much weight to the actual word choices.

Walter Levin says:

These things are never taught. People never talk about how you get along with each other in a group of four. And a group of four represents, more or less, a microcosm of our society: that, too, is something people never talk about. In short, you've got to learn it, but it's not taught, it's nothing that can be put in lessons.

\

REHEARSING FOR THE
SAKE OF FREEDOM

For Gregor Sigl, viola player of the Artemis Quartett, rehearsing, with all its constraints, is an essential precondition for maximum freedom in playing. I persuaded him to write about the rehearsal process of the Artemis Quartett:

'Es muss sein' – yes, it must be. There is no way around it. Musicians, in their quest for emotional dedication and ever more intensity, are well advised to exercise strategic thinking and to plan with cool heads – and to do this far enough in advance.

The first preparatory steps of a project are the nuts-and-bolts, the downright mundane parts of our work. This work starts ... in the office. As we draft our concert programmes with a lead time of three years or so, we need to think about a huge number of factors. There are programme cycles spanning more than one season, and scheduled CD recordings that need to be taken into account. We navigate our way between possible topical themes, various anniversaries and major tour plans. Agreements with important concert organisers play a role, as well as the projects of other quartet formations on the concert circuit – not to mention our own personal preferences and wishes.

Little by little, though, this abstract project activity transitions into the properly rewarding and emotionally satisfying stage of working. After the long incubation period, our relationship with the planned works, together with their programming contexts, becomes very personal, almost intimate. This is when we absorb the scores more and more comprehensively. They become part of our everyday life – until it feels like we have literally merged with them. During the final stage of preparing for the concert phase, it is as if our bodies move with the music: on our way to the rehearsal room, the music has already started, the sounds play in our heads. Each step on the staircase up to the train platform swings in the rhythm of the piece. And on the way back home, we catch ourselves absent-mindedly beating time to ourselves under the amused glances of giggling schoolchildren.

What is the process of those two to three years of preparation, more specifically? The foundation is built by continuous study of the score. Both confronting yourself with different recordings, and the quasi-inverted perspective of teaching, help to fill in the picture. During this time, your own ideas take shape, and a very specific tone of voice develops in your mind. Nuances of colour emerge in increasingly differentiated ways, and the phrasing is internalised. The first rehearsals often surprise us with that familiar feeling of belonging together. Having your own ideas affirmed by your colleagues makes for spontaneous happiness. We are amazed and delighted by our stylistic and emotional rapport. But, along with your excitement about some even more convincing nuance suggested by your colleagues, soon there's also surprise at the emergence of some completely contradictory standpoint. Divergences of this kind result either in heated discussions and determined efforts at persuasion, or in compliance with what appears to be the better argument. And then there is the occasional conciliatory yielding to a majority vote. What remains in the end, though, is the unreserved acceptance of whatever solution is found.

The rules are clear: every opinion has to be substantiated precisely, and derived from the structure and emotional development of the piece itself. The technical execution of any suggestion has to be demonstrated exactly. This kind of discipline helps in appreciating that an opinion that contradicts one's own approach is nevertheless of equal value – that one can understand it, accept it and internalise it. An authentic quartet interpretation is produced only if each of the four partners turns the results of the collective search into his or her own standpoint and his or her own feeling.

It is difficult enough for an individual to understand a major composition and to bring it to life. A quartet has the challenge of understanding the composition between the four of them, and of reaching the point where the four start to think and feel together. This merging of minds, hearts, senses and hands is extremely difficult and time-consuming. But ultimately, in my opinion, there is no more meaningful and profound form of making music than this sixteen-string foursomeness of feeling, experiencing and shaping.

In the first stage of rehearsals, we work meticulously through the entire work; the Artemis Quartett has, since its foundation three decades ago, spoken of this as the 'first wash cycle'. In the 'second wash cycle', we allow ourselves to play through individual movements and also try to get an overview of the piece as a whole. In this process, more and more details crystallise, and the view goes deeper. The horizon is broadening, too – the range of possibilities is becoming richer. Again and again, we play the work in its entirety. We make recordings of ourselves, listen to them individually and compile correction lists, which we work through together in the next rehearsals.

At some point, the countdown begins. A first private house concert is recorded on video. Together, we analyse the result. During the correction rehearsals, we prepare a second house concert. The 'actual' concert phase is preceded by a day of rest. Final preparation includes a one-and-a-half-hour rehearsal in the hall before each concert.

Our aim is to train ourselves in the procedure that we have worked out down to the tiniest detail, until everything becomes absolutely second nature to us. It is only at this point that the feeling of total freedom on stage sets in. The composers have created these worlds; they have prescribed our moves. But it is us – the four of us! – who perform them and fill them with life. We've planned for a long time and prepared meticulously. 'Es muss sein' – it must be. There really is no way around it. The highest intensity, though, calls for spontaneity – the unreserved here and now.

A FAREWELL TO
THE 'PRIMARIUS'

At the beginning of the nineteenth century, Europe's first professional quartets began to emerge [in Vienna]. One of them was the Schuppanzigh Quartet. Schuppanzigh was hired as a sixteen-year-old by Prince Lichnowsky to play quartets – Haydn quartets – in his residence. Beethoven would be there, listening, as Haydn rehearsed his quartets with this young group. Over the following decades, the Schuppanzigh Quartet premiered virtually all of Beethoven's string quartets, beginning with op. 18 (this time at the residence of Prince Lobkowitz, who commissioned the six op. 18 quartets) and ending with op. 135 – and almost every one of them in Beethoven's presence.

At that time, there were two quartets in Vienna. One of them was called the Schuppanzigh Quartet, the other, the Böhm Quartet. On one occasion, Beethoven was annoyed that one of his quartet works was not treated with due attention. He blamed Schuppanzigh and demanded that, from now on, the Böhm Quartet play it. Well, the only difference between the two groups was the first violinist: the three 'lower' players were almost always the same: Holz on the second violin, Weiss on the viola, and Linke on the cello. This had been the original Schuppanzigh Quartet, but when Schuppanzigh left Vienna for a number of years, Böhm took over as first violin. When Schuppanzigh returned to Vienna, one quartet became two.

Aren't people nowadays making their lives unnecessarily difficult?
There would be far less trouble if three people could just end up
deciding: we're the lower three voices, and we'll get ourselves different
first violinists to suit each programme. The same quartet could work
with half a dozen different first violinists – and the entire problem
would be settled. Those first violinists, all they've got to do is play the
violin, but the others, they've got to be able to play the quartet!

At this splendid idea, Walter Levin laughs impishly. As the first violinist
of a quartet for decades, he really knows what he is talking about.

I respond to this with the story of a late-night phone conversation I had
with the leader of a different quartet – let's call it the Mimosa Quartet.

HIM: 'I need a new violist.'

ME: 'Why, is he leaving?'

HIM: 'No, but I can't stand the sight of him any more, he
depresses me.'

(Pause.)

HIM: 'It was so nice this last summer, when he was ill, and
we had to play with substitutes. It was so inspiring – the
atmosphere was so good.'

ME: 'The new cellist – isn't he good?'

HIM: 'He is, but he's like the other two.'

ME: 'That's fine then. You're a quartet again.'

HIM: 'I need a new second violinist, and a different cellist, too.'

ME: 'So you need a new quartet.'

HIM: 'Yes. I always do.'

ME: 'So, you don't want to play as a quartet?'

HIM: 'I do.' [Thinks.] 'My quartet playing is so much better
with new people, I'm motivated.'

ME: '*Your* quartet playing is better?'

HIM: 'Yes, my quartet playing is better.'

ME: 'Well, well, *your* quartet playing is better. And what about the quartet, does it play better as well?'

HIM: 'My playing is better.'

ME: 'Alright, so I'll advertise the Mimosa Quartet from now on as follows: Arthur Mimosa – first violin. Second violin, viola and cello – subject to programme, dates (and whim). I'll include a photo of the quartet showing you and three faceless shadow-musicians. Maybe this is the real string quartet solution.'

Until about the middle of the twentieth century, quartets were mostly led by a 'Primarius', a violinist who would also be a well-known soloist. He hired and paid the three other musicians, who rarely got more than a fraction of the concert fees he collected for himself. As a matter of course, those quartets bore the names of their Primarius – he was the pivotal figure. It hardly mattered who the other three were, or even whether it was the same people playing each time.

Today's quartets vehemently object to the concept of the 'Primarius'. They prefer to speak of the 'first violinist', thus clarifying that he just plays the first voice of the score, and is not – beyond the role of his instrument – more important than the others. Today, egality is the rule, to such a degree that there are several string quartets in which the two violinists take turns playing first and second violin. There has been a considerable shift from the classical model of a group led by a single player. The definition of the string quartet according to the formula '4 × 1' is worlds apart from the old formula of '1 + 3'.

This, indeed, is evidence of the development of the string quartet genre, which has traced the course of political and social change over three centuries. And this, in turn, confirms the relentless modernity of string quartet music, and its standing as a form of art.

Günter Pichler again:

In every piece of music – apart from certain exceptions – the interplay of the leading voice and the accompanying ones is important, otherwise the listener won't understand the music. The more precisely the leading and the accompanying voices are presented to the listener – obviously only as one element of the interpretation, and along with inspired playing – the better the work reveals itself to him, and the more comfortable he feels. In a Bartók quartet, the challenge of each player taking the lead and playing a soloistic voice, too, is greater than in Haydn. The balance of voices in a Haydn or a Mozart quartet doesn't differ that much from the balance in a Bartók quartet, except that in Bartók, the lead travels from one instrument to the other, whereas in Haydn, it mostly stays with the first violin.

So, it's the composers who elicited equality, through the demands they made on the musicians. It's the composers who overturned the previously uncontested soloistic position of the Primarius. There are reasons to believe that composers didn't particularly concern themselves with the group-dynamic consequences of their creativity, and that these were not part of their artistic intention. What's certain, though, is that they absorbed the social spirit of their times, and worked it into their compositions – even if this wasn't their declared aim.

FINDING A NAME

A quartet is perceived as a quartet only if it has a name. People used to go to a Guarneri Quartet or an Alban Berg Quartett concert, not to a Michael Tree or Günter Pichler concert – just as now they would listen to the Quatuor Ébène or the Artemis Quartett, not to Pierre Colombet or to Gregor Sigl. The name by which concert-goers are attracted is already a public declaration of a commitment. The fact that a quartet bears a name is a matter of course, yet pondering the fact takes you to interesting conclusions. A quartet is only recognised as a quartet if it has a name. A sign, and by implication, a name, is a prerequisite of repetition, of the possibility of referring to something, repeatedly and in different contexts. Whereas founding a string quartet is the result of four individual decisions, finding a name can be seen as the first genuine decision made by the quartet as a whole. The name of the collective seals the promise of uniting forces in a joint project. But it also separates the collective from the individual: the collective identity pushes itself to the fore, blocking out the names of the people within it.

Hardly any aspiring young quartet player will be aware that his individual name will be outshone, that the fame of his own name will not grow in step with the quartet's successes. It also means that on their way to international recognition as musicians – as artists and as public figures – the four will not be seen any more with their very own identifying markers, their own names. Instead, people will, over time, talk of the Amadeus, the Guarneri, the Berg, the Tokyo, the Vogler, the Kuss, the Artemis and so on. It's always about 'the four', a unity in the plural.

One night at the opera, Eckart Runge was introduced by his own name to a British gentleman – who happened to be the newly appointed programme director at EMI London. During the dinner after the performance, this man asked Eckart what exactly he did for a living.

'I'm a cellist,' Eckart Runge replied, and then he added: 'Cellist of the Artemis Quartett.'

The man burst out in enthusiasm: 'You are the cellist of the Artemis Quartett?! Welcome to the EMI family!'

A week earlier, the Artemis Quartett had signed a contract with Virgin Classics/EMI.

Even knowledgeable string quartet aficionados, who may know entire discographies of certain string quartets by heart, might falter when asked the names of the individual members. Every 'string quartettist' knows that situation – when, in order to be recognised, he needs to give the name of his quartet and his instrument along with his own name.

Unlike a natural person, a string quartet is allowed to christen itself. Some choose the name of a city or a country, like the Cleveland Quartet or the Quartetto Italiano; some take it from foundations dedicated to particular composers, like the Zemlinsky Quartet or the Arnold Schönberg Quartet. This may be indicating an attachment to a certain place or institution, but may also be the more-or-less deliberate attempt to claim the position of ambassador or flagship for an institution, and to benefit from the possible privileges and material support this may bring.

Alban Berg, Ysaÿe, Arditti, Belcea, Carmina, Guarneri, Ébène, Cleveland, Tokyo, Cherubini, Amadeus, Juilliard, Artemis, Athena, Miró, Renoir, Modigliani, Rodin, Romantic, Panocha, Cremona: these are all names of quartets. Some names are self-explanatory, others may be confusing or baffling. Goddesses are invoked, mythical creatures, great heroes – or painters, even though no one knows whether they ever had any dealings with music. A composer's name, too, can be bewildering, especially if the composer in question never wrote a single quartet – only led one as a first violinist.

Inevitably, questions about the origin and meaning of names are part of the standard repertoire of media interviews of famous quartets. Luc-Marie Aguera, second violin of the now-defunct Quatuor Ysaÿe explains:

By choosing the name 'Quatuor Ysaÿe', we intended to honour a man who served music with enormous energy, shaping both the history of musical interpretation and the musical life of his time. Ysaÿe was a violinist, conductor and composer, and he founded his own string quartet. He inspired composers of the French School, Debussy, Franck, Chausson, Fauré, Saint-Saëns, d'Indy, Lekeu and others, who dedicated many works to him. Ysaÿe was the founding father of the Belgian-French violin school, which, together with St Petersburg, is one of the two great schools of violin playing, and to which violinists such as Carl Flesch, Jacques Thibaud, Henryk Szeryng, Max Rostal and Arthur Grumiaux were proud to belong. We understand the choosing of his name as an homage to the charisma, artistic versatility and never-tiring curiosity of a man who always stood up for the music of his time.

Evi Levin, on the naming of the LaSalle Quartet:

In autumn 1946, Robert Mann, first violinist of the young Juilliard Quartet, tried to cancel a lunchtime concert in New Jersey. He called the lady from the Tuesday Musicale and explained to her that although his quartet couldn't accept the engagement, he would recommend another ensemble to her who could play in their place. He made the long-distance call from a phone booth in the drug store near his Manhattan apartment. So soon after the war, private phones were still rather rare.

'What's the name of the quartet you're recommending?', the lady asked. Robert Mann knew that a student quartet without a name would never get an engagement. Hesitating, he looked for a moment at the street signs he could see from the phone booth in the drug store, which was on Broadway and LaSalle, and he said: 'LaSalle.'

That was the baptism of the LaSalle Quartet by Robert Mann in autumn 1946. Good for him that he didn't say the Broadway Quartet ...

Robert Mann didn't say the Levin Quartet either, a name that would obviously have suited the quartet well, considering its first violinist, who was graced with a strong character. The four musicians, including Walter Levin, decided to keep the name that was given to them by Robert Mann. It certainly doesn't refer in any way to the biography of René-Robert Cavelier, Sieur de La Salle, the seventeenth-century French Catholic missionary, adventurer and fur trader, who is said to have explored the Mississippi region and after whom the street in New York is named – *that* LaSalle never dealt with art or music. And three of the four musicians of the quartet were New York German-Jewish immigrants.

There are no rules for picking a name, only limitations: for example, if the name that has been chosen by the quartet is contested by an outside party. There can be moving stories behind the choice of names, and also simple, rational facts; it can be down to strategic calculation or sincere acknowledgement, a lack or abundance of imagination, cluelessness or opportunity. Whether it's chosen for political, musical, natural or accidental reasons, the name becomes part and parcel of the history of the quartet. It stands for a repertoire, a sound, a direction, a school – in short, for a single public and artistic person.

ES MUSS SEIN!

The day-to-day life of a musician is like a meticulously woven tapestry made up of commitments, responsibilities, arrangements and absolutely unalterable dates. To have a musician appear on stage at the right time, in the right venue, on the day announced months in advance, is the result of years of planning and highly detailed organisation on the part of the promoter, the agent and the artist. This is obviously even more true of string quartets. There are cases – as in the famous example of Evi Levin, wife of the first violinist of the LaSalle Quartet – where a fifth person takes on the task of administering all internal and external affairs for the group. Otherwise, every responsibility – and there are so many – stays with the musicians themselves.

Who keeps track of which works are going to being played when, and how much rehearsal time is to be allotted to each work? Who sets up the necessary rehearsal schedules for everyone?

Who keeps in touch with the agency, updates the joint calendar, keeps records of all outstanding questions, and makes sure that they are discussed and that the agency gets feedback?

Who manages the communications with composers and benefactors? Who does the interviews? Who goes through the edits for the latest recording, writing comments and sending them to the sound engineer?

Decisions about travel plans must be made. The tax authorities want to see certain documents. Sheet music must be organised, pictures from the latest photo shoot selected, visas applied for – individually. It doesn't take too much imagination to picture what's involved when four people, probably each with different ideas, look to settle the stack of questions large and small that pave the path of everyday life: Should we get the eight-thirty train, because one of us prefers to arrive early and take a rest before the rehearsal? Or maybe the nine-thirty instead, because another one is more of a late riser and doesn't need a nap? Common sense says let everyone travel as they please. The reality is, because of costs or plain habit, they reach an agreement and travel together.

Will it be possible to include Schubert's great String Quartet in G major in the repertoire for the season after next, to allow the quartet to join a prestigious 'Schubertiade'[11] concert series? The slots for large-scale works are already fixed; it would be possible only if we drop Dvořák's A flat major quartet, but that has been on the cellist's wish list for a very long time. Or would it somehow be possible to find a way of doing both pieces?

The organiser of the upcoming concert has, at short notice, issued a dinner invitation for afterwards. As it happens, everyone has already made their own plans, but it would be rude to decline the invitation entirely. Who sacrifices their private appointment and undertakes to represent the quartet?

What about ties? Should they all be the same, or the same but in different colours, or should they all perform in black T-shirts anyway? Is it absolutely necessary to dress identically, or should the outfits just coordinate? This discussion can get even more interesting and more intri-

---

11 'Schubertiade' is the title of a number of music festivals and concert series commemorating the legendary musical events that were more or less formally organised by the friends of Franz Schubert, where Schubert would play his own music.

cate with female quartets: dress, skirt or trousers? Glamorous or plain?

There has been an agreement – now considered a rule – that overseas tours should be limited to two and a half weeks, because with long flights, the travel time can add up to three weeks. Now, there's a request from the US: would it be possible to make an exception for the tour season after next – which would be in two years' time? If not, it won't be possible to squeeze in a date for Montreal, and the organiser might end up being terribly disappointed. When do you start making exceptions – and how do you decide what happens in two years' time?

Does the quartet accept an invitation for a concert in Israel, even though the news suggests again and again that a trip there is risky? One of the members thinks that there's danger everywhere and that people in such countries might be particularly hungry for music; another has little children and doesn't want to worry his family more than necessary.

One member makes all his decisions unambiguously and with lightning speed, but revises his reasoning a few days later. A second member can never make up his mind at all, and always demands explanations for the tiniest detail. He carries on balancing pros and cons until the initial question has evaporated and problems of a completely different kind have emerged. The third brings the general question of the number and duration of rehearsals – which, as far as he is concerned, are always insufficient – into every discussion. And the fourth has the talent of recognising the only possible, real solution, but only when it's too late and a limping compromise has already had to be made.

And sometimes things are completely different – but just as complicated.

The world of chamber music proceeds deliberately – a flash in the pan doesn't go down well there. When the name of the Artemis Quartett suddenly became known to a wider audience in 1997, after it had won no less than two big competitions, the quartet had already been in existence for eight years. A string quartet pushes its way through very slowly, rather like a tortoise. Like a tortoise, too, it carries its home around with itself – its shell is its musical home, where it always stays – and within itself, leaving all outside things outside. Obviously, each concert hall is different, each acoustic is special, each audience is new. The chairs are not always suitable, and the welcome can be more friendly or less friendly. But once the four are in front of their stands (mostly they bring their own), they are on familiar territory. They don't have to deal with an orchestra or with a – sometimes grumpy – conductor.

It's not primarily the idea of entering a partnership for life that is at the origin of a quartet; it's more the particular form of making music that challenges individuality and banishes loneliness. Protected by the shell of the quartet, the life partnership develops almost imperceptibly. Only much later do the interpersonal relationships and social structures that have evolved come to the fore – and sometimes become the source of problems.

There are quartets that are led almost dictatorially by one member, who decides all musical and organisational matters – these are most often the quick quartets! And then there are decidedly democratic quartets, in which no one is able to make whatever minuscule or unimportant decision is required for the ensemble without coordinating with all the others – these are frequently the very slow quartets. And, in between, there is an infinite number of possible methods of self-organisation.

One could imagine a promising distribution of roles where the single authority, which in the old days was given to the 'Primarius', is divided into a multitude of 'partial authorities'. These could emerge naturally out of the respective musical or other talents of the members. There might be the one who is particularly influential in musical matters, who is recognised unquestioningly by all three others as a kind of guiding spirit, but who is out of touch with and never cares about any kind of practical reality. Another one, in contrast, might be a superb master of his instrument, and be irreplaceable for the ensemble, but might not have any personal ambition of leading musically. Instead, he could be a skilful manager, familiar with the latest communication technology, versatile in dealing with concert organisers, and eager to take the initiative in promoting the quartet's career. The third one might not be particularly keen to claim either role, but maybe what he would love in the quartet's life would be the stage and the public. He would turn out to be a gifted entertainer, a popular and engaging social animal. And, finally, there'd be the quiet one, who'd love to keep lists and be a passionate collector. So, he'd be the one taking care of the well-organised quartet archive and the music library, checking and paying the bills, filing the receipts and keeping meticulous records of the repertoire they play.

In reality, though, talents and qualities are never defined and distributed in such distinct ways. And not everyone is necessarily equally aware that they are part of a collective. When there was still the 'Primarius', everything was pretty easy: he *was* the quartet, externally and internally, and in all possible respects. He made decisions, more or less dictatorially, on dates, programmes and fees. However, in an association on equal terms, a union based on equality, the quartet itself is the supreme authority. This requires consensus – which is not to be confused with the rule of the majority. Consensus means that decisions that are made should, as often as possible, allow each member to identify individually with them and to act on them as their own.

The quartet is an ideal example of democracy in practice, as the four consider themselves as partners on an equal footing in every respect. This doesn't necessarily mean that everyone has to be capable of doing everything! I'm speaking here from bitter experience as a string quartet agent. The idea of democracy, held in high esteem by many quartets – an idea that sounds good and raises the quartet to the level of role model for society in general – does require that the four regard themselves as

equal partners. But it does not imply that everyone can manage everything, and it certainly doesn't imply that they *do* manage everything. In a
democracy, too, responsibility must be delegated, and for this, individual
talent is more important than the idea of equal sharing.

In musical matters, the mutual criticism within a quartet can be
quite abrasive, precisely because the four members feel equivalent to
each other. In other areas, they deal with each other in ways that are
much more careful, sometimes proving patient and forbearing over long
periods, even if the consequences are not easy to take. It took me a
long time to understand that this kind of tolerance and support is no
contradiction to the intransigence that they show in musical matters.
It's the proof of an uncompromisingly professional community that,
nevertheless, allows for human shortcomings.

Arguing for democracy means arguing for the idea of fairness. Yet, in
many cases, democracy is invoked just to avoid confronting the topic of
authority. Authority – not to be confused with authoritarian behaviour –
is ostensibly not reconcilable with equality. (It is clearly reconcilable
with the idea of equivalence of different talents.) Flatly rejecting
authority would certainly allow the rejection of authoritarian behaviour,
but it would also downgrade consensus to the level of compromise. A
compromise is nothing but the lowest common denominator, neither
inspiring nor satisfying. Consensus, in contrast, is the volition that has
been achieved together, the inner force of the quartet, the engine of
success. Here, authority is indispensable. It fuels the necessary efforts
of persuasion and it sparks creative confrontation. It indicates direction
and brings clarity, and makes decisions possible.

Walter Levin says:

A quartet has to learn to cope with difficulties. Just walking away, just
breaking up, that's easy, anyone can do that. That's not an art. The art

is keeping it together. If someone is a wimp and reacts to the first real problem, whatever it may be, by saying 'Thanks, I'm out' – this person shouldn't have started playing in a string quartet in the first place. There will always be problems of some kind. A problem means it's high time to talk properly and precisely again together as a foursome. That's the ground rule. You've got to learn that. It should be part of teaching string quartets: learning how to cope with problems. And not by saying, 'Either we do it this way, or I quit.' Threatening to leave is taboo! The only thing you mustn't do is say 'I'm out.' Because if you do that, the quartet is kaput anyway, there's no need to talk any more.

Raphaël Merlin on the same topic:

Once they reach the prime of life – that is, after they have successfully managed their initial unification and then accomplished the enormous work of finding an appropriate distance from each other for living their lives – mature quartets, or 'career quartets', seem to have found a solid way through, a cruising speed. We cannot say whether the path is a narrow footway or more like a motorway, but what is really striking is that the more it is travelled, the further away its destination seems. This is for a very simple reason: in the permanent molecular motion that proves the quartet is alive, nothing is complete. Each is already, by nature, split, since each musician is both an artist and a craftsman, a designer and a builder, a leader and a follower, a transmitter and a receiver. (This could possibly be the definitive definition of a chamber musician: one who sends and receives at the same time, in the way that jazz musicians who practise 'interplay' do.) This makes the dialogue ever-ephemeral. The search for a common vocabulary never comes to a full stop, because it seems that the individual personalities evolve invisibly, and faster than the group itself.

The chronic precariousness of this professional model, the relative fragility of the alliance, rests just as much on a schism within each member. Each is made up of his sticking power and his safety equipment. It is very important that each one tells himself, more or less consciously, that he always retains his freedom to leave the group at any moment. It is a bit of an abstract safety – a virtual security blanket, a parachute that not only allows the individual to pursue his own artistic path, but also permits him to express his positive energy for the group or to be one of its driving forces. In sum: by telling myself that I'm staying because I know that I can leave at any moment, I have my life jacket, or my ejection seat. An illusion, but fundamental. In this way, it's not exactly a contract of marriage. It's more like a confession of faith, a tacit pact.

Several times during my eighteen years in the quartet, I have felt myself to be at the end of my tether. I particularly remember our Bartók recording in 2006. During one break, I stared at myself in the mirror and swore that as soon as this living torture was over, I would leave the group.

I developed split personality symptoms: I kept finding myself in situations where I felt caught between the quartet and my private life. I'm not sure whether I have ever 'returned' to the quartet, but it's true there have been times – the relatively carefree times – when my reservations have relaxed.

Basically, it is always the same things that reconcile you to your vocation: the repertoire, the recognition, the intensity of life, adventure, brotherhood, the power of forgiveness, the fascination of the inevitable slowness of this progress that is both collective and individual, and the feeling of being part of something that goes far beyond yourself and gives you more than you could ever achieve by yourself.

UNSAID, YET TANGIBLE

Each of our artists is accompanied on his or her travels by what we in the agency call *O-Karten*, short for *Organisationskarten* (organisation cards). On these cards, every single detail for every single concert will be listed in a schedule that is accurate to the minute. When everything was still done manually and life didn't need to fit into a smartphone, *O-Karten* were printed on light card stock and sent to the artists by post. *O-Karten* always offered a welcome excuse for an argument of greater or lesser ferociousness – they would either arrive at the last minute, or so early that crucial points that only emerged later would have to be scribbled in by hand. Because they served as the perfect outlet for whatever frustrations would come up, they ended up cementing the relationship between us and the artists.

In response to our artists' comments and suggestions, we had kept tinkering over the years, trying to find the perfect size and shape for these *O-Karten*. For instance, for the gentlemen of the Alban Berg Quartett, it was of vital importance that they would fit, bound into a little book, into the inner pockets of their jackets. Every bit of information relevant to a concert had to be visible at a glance.

The question of *which* bits of information – the day, the time, the location, the programme, etc. – had to be listed, and where, was a perennial topic for discussion. It's the same today, even if it's a long time since *O-Karten* were produced in any physical sense. If anything went pear-shaped, it was (obviously!) only because our *O-Karten* were wrong or clumsily put together. It was never because our artists hadn't read them carefully enough. With smartphone screens even more cramped for space than physical cards, these problems have only got worse.

The *O-Karte* was and still is the frame within which a relationship with an artist is woven – an ongoing creative process in at least three dimensions. A very important instrument.

Having worked for artists for four decades now, I sometimes take a step back and reflect on how the relationship between agent and artist has changed, and what might have been the most important drivers of this process. Without any doubt, one driver has been the availability of enormously flexible and budget-friendly means of travel. This has not only contributed a great deal to the globalisation of artists' careers, but it has also massively stoked up the rhythm of their concert schedules, and the total number of concerts has increased without any regard to geographically sensible planning. But as far as the relationship between agents and artists is concerned, general digitalisation has changed things in a much more dramatic way. In the past, it was extremely unusual for artists to book trips or hotels by themselves. They might have had special requirements that we knew about, and we would arrange their tour schedules accordingly. Today, faced with any question of logistics, artists can take care of themselves – they can be their own best travel agencies. The result is that many of the more delicate situations that used to require our help no longer arise. But these were the very situations affording us glimpses of some deeply private matters, situations which, by their nature, demanded discretion. Discretion is a very delicate coat for a relationship, and in a way it's a pity that it is not required any more. Not everything had to be put into words or explained, but what was kept unsaid lent a certain substance to the atmosphere. With self-sufficiency, the artist can guard his privacy more carefully, but what is lost in this supposed autonomy are all the things that were unsaid yet tangible. As a result, there is a certain encapsulation, a form of distancing.

I was just about to take a closer look at this phenomenon, to investigate what it is that has replaced the delicate matter of discretion in the modern world, when the coronavirus pandemic struck and paralysed everything for months. At the time of writing, there is no end in sight. We are in the middle of a crisis that is shaking up the music world and turning everything that used to be true upside down.

Currently, it is not possible to travel at will: there are no longer so many flights from A to B that one could easily play one evening in A and the next in B. Long-forgotten natural obstacles require careful and very flexible planning once more.

In this crisis, the artists' needs are changing again – as is the agent's role. It would be premature, by far, to draw any conclusions from all this, or even to identify the true questions that are being exposed by this great earthquake. There will be many, I am sure.

TILL DEATH DO US PART

Forty years of the Guarneri Quartet! On the evening of 17 January 2004, on the occasion of the closing ceremony of the 26th National Conference of Chamber Music America in New York, speeches were made, and gratitude was expressed for the countless wonderful concerts the Guarneris had played and were – at that time – still playing around the globe. And then the entrance: five gentlemen stepped on to the stage – and played the C major String Quintet by Franz Schubert. All five of them were the Guarneri Quartet. David Soyer, the founding cellist, was all of seventy-eight years old, significantly older than his colleagues. He had decided, after thirty-seven years of playing with the Guarneri, that living the life of a travelling artist had become too exhausting, and that he would like to devote himself more intensively to teaching. The quartet had chosen a worthy successor – Peter Wiley, a former student of David Soyer's, who had already made his mark as a chamber musician on the international stage.

They had decided to have a transition period during which Peter Wiley took over many of their concerts, David Soyer playing only a few. And again and again, the Schubert quintet, in which both cellists performed, was on the programme – a handover, as it were. An outstanding example of a successful change of cast in a string quartet.

The decision of four people to take on life as a string quartet is not unlike a vow of marriage, being unlimited in time and mutual in its commitment – even if it's not formally made in front of a civil or religious authority. Quite frequently, quartets are depicted in this manner: *Ehe zu viert* ('Marriage in a foursome') was the title of a TV portrait of the Alban Berg Quartett.

Until well into the twentieth century, civil marriage was often not a matter of free choice. Certain conditions had to be met: pedigree, social class, religious confession and financial endowment had to match. Marriage was not the result of romantic love, and was often determined by others, mostly the parents. Its purpose was to foster and preserve traditional values, and it was not intended for the pleasure or the personal fulfilment of the individuals involved. Above all, a marriage served the family, the protection of the blood line, the name. Respect, dignity, trust and the economic basis were the guarantors and pillars of a marriage.

The string quartet could be regarded as the ideal example of a traditional marriage in this sense. It is not primarily love for each other that unites the four; it's the love for the cause. And so, the basis of the bond lies outside the association. The players don't form a string quartet because they love each other, but because they see appropriate partners in each other, and because, together, they can satisfy their passion for this special kind of music. Music is the reason for learning how to deal with each other, for really getting to know each other, for accepting and respecting each other, and eventually for setting up some kind of life partnership together. Its aim is not to live together in a harmonious way, it is to work – and this can include robust and passionate exchanges. What they share and foster as a group is what is visible from the outside: their profession, their talent and their ambition. They're united by the music, and by what music gives to them and makes of them. Although they may meet only as adults, they share – retrospectively – a piece of their childhoods: music will have played a central role in all their lives from an early age; it will have distinguished them from other children, isolated them, or brought them together with others. They come from different worlds, but they share a language of the 'before'. A friendship that maybe was seminal for the joint project, or even love, arising – sometimes surreptitiously, sometimes retrospectively – out of the long journey they end up sharing: these things are part of the private aspect of the quartet.

Sometimes it is literally death that ends the life of a quartet. Many string quartet followers will remember their distress when the news of the sudden death of Peter Schidlof, the violist of the Amadeus Quartet, spread like wildfire in the world of chamber music. Norbert Brainin, Siegmund Nissel, Peter Schidlof and Martin Lovett had been the Amadeus Quartet for forty years. The gentlemen had admittedly reached an age at which most people retire, but they had not yet considered ending the quartet's career – at least, there was nothing to suggest this filtering through to the public. Concerts had been planned, as well as various celebratory activities to mark the occasion of their fortieth anniversary season.

When Norbert Brainin was asked a little later whether they would carry on, he replied that there was no repertoire for two violins and a cello. Several weeks later, an – unforgettable – memorial concert was organised in Paris, during which three members of the Alban Berg Quartett and the three remaining members of the Amadeus Quartet played Brahms' String Sextet no. 2, and the Scherzo from the String Sextet no. 1 for their deceased colleague. The concert could only be advertised under the title 'Members of the Amadeus Ensemble and Members of the Alban Berg Quartett'. The Amadeus Quartet had died with Peter Schidlof.

String quartets are not only private associations: they are public persons, too. This is why, in the case of changes in the line-up, the outside world feels concerned and reacts. During the first three to five years of a quartet's life, changes are relatively common. The public barely notices, and if it does, it shows understanding for young people's changing decisions. However, if it's a well-known quartet, the outside world pricks up its ears and is worried. During the process of separation, the individuals come to the fore again. Even if the names of the individual players are not too familiar to the audience, the quartet itself is perceived as a kind of stable image. If someone leaves, this image changes. The name of the leaving member and the name of the new member, along with their instrument, suddenly take centre stage.

A certain sensationalism might play a role here, too. People want to understand, they want an explanation for what made the association split up. As long as the quartet has performed annually or every other year in the familiar cast, it is seen as a paradigm. People almost forget that a quartet consists of four individuals, who as well as playing music together also have to get along with each other – and who sometimes simply get to the point where they can't. Once a change is announced, the public gets involved in the internal upheaval; it intrudes into the quartet's private sphere. Suddenly, there's room for involvement. One of the first things is that confidence in the quartet is spontaneously withdrawn. 'The audience', represented by the promoters who engage the musicians, is given – or claims – the right to judge whether the choice of the new quartet member is adequate for the standard of the ensemble and for the image everyone has of the quartet.

If a member tells a quartet that he or she is going to leave, the quartet must think about a number of questions. Sometimes they ask me: Do we advertise to get as many applicants as possible for the position? Or is our search for a new member better carried out by following our personal connections and those of our closest friends? Does one approach possible candidates under conditions of confidentiality? How should we handle the public? Deny all rumours until a new member is found? Or deal with the news openly, and let the public take part in everything?

The musicians who plan to leave the quartet, too, face a lot of questions: What is the right moment to tell the others about the decision? Before the Munich concert? After the Paris concert? How long will someone have to continue playing after declaring his decision? Is it possible to carry on at all? Are there possible legal entanglements?

This is where the similarities between a string quartet and a marriage are particularly striking – both with respect to the behavioural patterns inside the 'relationship' that is breaking up, and with respect to the reactions of the outside world. Nowadays, a separation is still painful, but involves none of the feelings of disgrace that used to be involved in a divorce – or, indeed, in a quartet separation. Separations do leave scars, but they no longer leave a stigma. A new member offers new approaches and new chances, and brings into question solidified or even calcified routines. A new language is invented. The group, then, is in a state which is best described as falling in love.

EMBERS AND ICE

―――――

For me [says Eckart Runge, cellist of the Artemis Quartett], *there are two things, both equally important, that make the quartet the consummate musical form.*

There's the glorious repertoire, to start with. Composers from all periods wrote arguably their most beautiful and, without question, their most advanced works for this line-up. That's because of the abstract nature of its form: four equal voices, as capable of homogeneity as of heterogeneity, far removed from any social glamour (very different from the solo concerto). For most composers, this made the string quartet not only a field of experimentation, but also the ideal form through which to express their deepest and most personal feelings.

I feel the human factor in the quartet is as appealing as its repertoire. You're a team where you share responsibility – you take on responsibility, and you hand it over. Authority is a liquid that flows: you can't grab it and keep it for yourself, nor can you easily push it away. This makes possible an intense identification with the whole, and, at the same time, it releases more creative potential than would ever be possible within a rigid structure like, for example, an orchestra, with its hierarchical organisation. With the quartet's flexible structure, you become a completely irreplaceable part of the whole, with total

―――――

responsibility, but without ever being alone. In my eyes, this is an ideal
model – the almost utopian ideal of a well-functioning community. Of
course, it's not always easy to channel centrifugal energies, and to turn
differences of opinion into joint positions. But for me, it's one of the
most wonderful challenges ever – to keep on trying to make this work.

An ode to the string quartet! Eckart Runge wrote this in 2006, at my request. I wanted then for him to be the young voice in this book, the voice following on from those of the doyens Walter Levin and Günter Pichler. Also, here was the cello – not the first violin – speaking in the first person for all four, an eloquent and positive sign of how things are moving on after the end of the 'Primarius' era.

In 1997, I took on the representation of the Artemis Quartett. That's when I became the fifth member of the band, as it were. At that time, I didn't know what 'being the fifth' would really mean in this particular case – which was lucky.

My story with the Artemis Quartett had begun about two years earlier, soon after they started working with Walter Levin in Lübeck. They were due to give a concert in Hamburg.

Walter had urgently (too urgently) asked me (ordered me) to go there. My children were still small, I felt stressed, and I was reluctant because I felt that Walter Levin was just being too demanding. The concert was on a Sunday morning at eleven. I did go – grumpily. I had wished to be doing something different that Sunday. I wasn't prepared for what was to come: the young Artemis Quartett literally knocked me over. There was such energy bursting out of them, their tempos were so fast! It was too much for me. I was annoyed, and my bad temper was only made worse by such an abundance of unrestrained positive power. When I got home, I wrote to Walter Levin that I couldn't work for the quartet: it was just too much of everything for me, too alien.

In September 1996, the Artemis Quartett won the ARD competition[12] and Eckart Runge wrote me a letter. It was the first of the many letters he sent to me over the years, all so characteristic of him. The missive didn't come without a certain edge. It included both a hint that Eckart knew about my letter to Walter Levin, and a carefully wrapped-up demand that they, the quartet, be accepted now – after this great internationally recognised success – into the ranks of quartets that I represented, and to which they now demonstrably belonged.

However, that got me into a quagmire. I had a commitment with the Borciani competition, which was to take place a few months later. I was to be responsible for a major tour for the winners – who, of course, had not yet been nominated. I couldn't possibly bring two award-winning string quartets 'to market' at the same time, so I was obliged to decline the Artemis Quartett's request. Whereupon the quartet decided to submit themselves to the ordeal of a competition one more time and registered for the Borciani competition. It was a highly dangerous thing to do. If you win first prize at one of the most famous competitions in classical music, you should leave it at that. You should not risk doing less well in another competition of high but not quite as high reputation. What if you don't win another first prize? That could even devalue the original one.

But the Artemis Quartett wanted the tour that came with winning the Borciani Prize, and they wanted to be on the same list as the other big names! They played, and they won. The question of representing them was no longer a question.

So, within a few months, they had won two of the most important

12 An international classical music competition, run since 1952, on behalf of the German public broadcasters in the ARD (*Arbeitsgemeinschaft der öffentlich-rechtlichen Rundfunkanstalten der Bundesrepublik Deutschland* – Cooperative of Broadcasters in Public Service of the Federal Republic of Germany).

string quartet competitions. As you might expect, the world of chamber music was clamouring to hear them. And what did they do? They asked the world to wait for them for a full year. They still wanted to work with the Alban Berg Quartett in Vienna, and they wanted to work properly, not just to squeeze in the odd lesson before or after exhausting concert tours. This was unheard of, and defending it convincingly was quite a challenge for me as their agent. But the world *did* wait for them – and then the world was thrilled with them. The two violinists led alternately, which was very controversial for many organisers – this didn't affect them either. Everything was successful: the concerts, the record contracts, the papers praised them to the skies.

The Artemis Quartett was the outstanding, spectacularly successful young string quartet of the late 1990s, a shining example of perfection, strength and innovation. They glittered like pop stars on posters and on record covers that were revolutionary for the time, with the Berlin of the turn of the millennium as their backdrop. Their reach went far beyond the narrow confines of chamber music.

Exactly ten years earlier, the Carmina Quartet had been the first of my quartets whose members were in the same age bracket as me. And now, here was the Artemis Quartett, and I was noticeably older than they were. That was, again, an entirely new situation for me. I was expected to know how one does things, to have answers to every question. Which was only partially the case. It's true, I knew how 'one' did things in lots of respects, but the 'ones' in these situations were representatives of the older generation – older than me, and therefore much older than the members of the Artemis. These young quarteteers had a different kind of respect for that generation, which was more like that of their grandparents. They confidently claimed the right to shape their own future, whether the establishment liked it or not. I quickly realised that I was not the one setting the standards, but that instead I would have to follow the quartet and put their standards into practice. It was as if I was always having to learn the same lesson, either from my elders, or from my peers, and now, from the young ones: as the 'fifth' member of a quartet, you're neither in nor out. It's a position which, in a crisis, requires total dedication, but otherwise a certain distance and discretion, so as not to constrict, so as simply to follow.

The crisis-ridden history of the Artemis Quartett is laid out in detail in the press and in documentaries: Wilken Ranck, violinist of the original group, had already left by the time I got to know the quartet. Violist Volker Jacobsen and violinist Heime Müller left in 2007, and Natalia Prishepenko, the other founding violinist, in 2012. Eckart Runge remained as the only founding member, as, over time, new members joined: Gregor Sigl, violinist (at least at first), viola Friedemann Weigle and violin Vineta Sareika. When Friedemann Weigle took his own life in 2015, Gregor Sigl took his place as the viola in the quartet, playing Friedemann's very instrument, while Anthea Kreston took the second violin position. Finally, in 2019, Eckart Runge and Anthea Kreston left the Artemis. Harriet Krigh now plays the cello, while Suyeon Kim plays violin alongside Vineta Sareika, and Gregor Sigl remains on the viola.

The procession of a total of eleven names in these few breathless lines gives some idea of the earthquakes the Artemis Quartett has lived through.

In 2006, when he wrote his beautiful ode to the quartet for me, Eckart Runge had no clue that half a year later no fewer than two of his colleagues would leave the quartet, or that this turnover of personnel was destined to become something like the trademark of the Artemis Quartett. Thirteen years later, Eckart Runge himself, the last founding member, left the Artemis. After three packed, eventful decades, he decided to take a different path, to stop subordinating everything to the quartet, and to use his everyday life for other forms of music.

When someone has the courage to give up almost everything that has formed his identity in order to embark, in his early fifties, on a new adventure, one can really only be jealous. And in the complicated and not particularly tolerant musical world, Eckart's had been a position that was very much admired. When he told me of his decision to leave in the early summer of 2018, I was angry. And I was full of sympathy. And I was jealous. All at the same time.

Nobody could have blamed him – at least, no one with an inkling of what it means to devote thirty years of one's life to an idea, let alone to the extraordinarily demanding Artemis Quartett. But why now? Why not five years earlier, when the great multiple catastrophes crashed over the quartet and the whole world would have felt the deepest sympathy?

In the summer of 2015, when Friedemann Weigle took his own life, Eckart Runge was undergoing chemotherapy. If he had said then that he was calling it a day, there is no doubt that I would have spent hours, days even, in tears – for him, for Friedemann, for the quartet and thus also for myself – trying to write a sad yet dignified farewell statement to send out to the whole musical world. Perhaps something like this: 'After the tragic suicide of Friedemann Weigle, the wonderful Artemis Quartett has been laid to rest with him.'

But this is not what happened. At the time, it was particularly important to Eckart not to give up after Friedemann's death, and to save the quartet from the deep hole it was in. It seems he needed to achieve this before he could truly draw a line for himself.

I can't really explain what it's like for someone who is neither an insider nor an outsider to be part of all this, sharing it and enduring it. These things can only be lived. Right after Eckart, Anthea Kreston, the new second violin, announced her departure too. That was the moment when the thought came into my head that now I could go as well. Surely, now the quartet was going to disintegrate. And after twenty years of sailing on the high seas, I was overwhelmed by an urge to leave the boat. But when Vineta Sareika and Gregor Sigl said that no matter what, they would carry on with the Artemis Quartett, and so would look for two new members, I spent a long night struggling with myself. I decided umpteen times to tell them both, first thing in the morning, that my decision was to quit as well. But this is what I did not do. It would have been a betrayal – and probably the death blow – to the quartet. They were courageously defying fate. It was not up to me to make this decision for them; I had to go along with it. And this was exactly right.

There has never been a quartet that has made its 'fourness' so abstract in this way. No other quartet has ever set such a brilliant example of how tightly entwined intimacy and alienation can be: embers and ice. No other quartet has proved to be so independent of its individual members, even when each one is so outstanding that the quartet would be unthinkable without him or her during their respective times.[13]

---

13 In May 2021 – a few months after the new German edition of this book appeared – the Impresariat Simmenauer issued a press release that read: 'Dear friends of the string quartet, the Artemis Quartett has decided to take a leave of absence from playing for an indefinite period. After one setback too many, in an already turbulent time, difficult for all of us, it is at present impossible for the quartet to plan reliably. Therefore, our 24-year-long intense collaboration with the Artemis Quartett is also coming to an end. Our joint history, shaped by great success but also by dramatic blows of fate, formed an remarkably close relationship between the musicians and Impresariat Simmenauer. We thank all members of the Artemis Quartett for this inspiring journey!'

FAREWELL AND A NEW START

Arnold Steinhardt, first violinist of the Guarneri Quartet, and Valentin Erben, cellist of the Alban Berg Quartett, are both in town for a week. They're teaching at the summer school of the Hamburg conservatoire. It's an odd situation. Both quartets have announced that they will be retiring: the Alban Berg Quartett in the summer of 2008, the Guarneri Quartet one year later. They were my first two quartets, and now they are leaving the stage, after twenty-five years of working with me. They are quitting of their own accord; some of them are far beyond normal retirement age. There is no drama. The ending is going to be nice: a farewell celebration. Many tears will be shed. People will flock to the concerts, which will be advertised as last concerts in every town. It will be a big turning point for chamber music, with two giants of the string quartet stage leaving at almost the same time.

On Friday, I have arranged to meet Arnold for coffee. It's the first time I've seen him face to face since the announcement. There is a short moment of mutual unfamiliarity: we don't really know each other on a personal level, although we've known each other well and for a long time in our respective functions as quartet violinist and agent. There have been difficult times, wide-ranging conversations. They would come to Europe each year; we would normally meet once during their tour and have dinner after a concert. Sometimes, there would be months of silence between us, only letters or faxes being exchanged, sometimes after long intervals. The musicians of the Guarneri Quartet have always been completely down-to-earth artists. They've always been straightforward in their dealings, reliable in their opinions, and firm in their tastes and habits. They have always known their way around, and whenever anything extraordinary would happen, one of the musicians would call me, then, most often, another one shortly after that, but very rarely all four of them.

We talk about the end of the quartet. Arnold says the time they have been allowed to experience as a quartet and as musicians has been a blessed one. Today, he wouldn't really want to start out as a musician; it's such a tough world out there. He considers himself lucky. He has written a book about his quartet, another one about playing the violin. He wants to be around for much longer, even without the quartet – for him, there's so much to say and to do. It's a friendly, even cheerful conversation, and yet – later, in the evening – I become wistful. It is the beginning of an ending.

The following Tuesday, I meet Valentin. We amble up the road, find a café and sit outside on the terrace. In an otherwise quite rainy summer, it has turned out to be a nice afternoon. We talk about a sextet project with the Arditti Quartet in two years' time, and about what it's going to be like without his own quartet. Valentin launches into a grand sentence: 'Oh, you know, the quartet, that's, erm, that's ... well, erm, difficult ... terrible ... oh, just wonderful!' So many sentiments, so many feelings – an entire lifetime is resonating. We keep quiet for a while.

He carries on musing: 'Actually, the string quartet, the way we're living it, is a contradiction. Messrs Haydn and Beethoven certainly didn't imagine that four musicians would ever team up around their string quartets in a permanent way, or travel around the world with their works, and share an entire life around them. No, certainly not. Their music was most probably intended to be used for social gatherings, along the lines of Goethe's much-quoted comment, "You are listening in on a conversation between four sensible people."'

I realise that I am seeing Valentin differently now. After all these years that I've been in charge of him as a 'quartettist', now, he is emerging as an individual. I am amazed: I have known all these people for such a long time! I thought I knew them, but it seems that all I really knew was their roles in the quartet – a large portion of their lives and of their personalities, but not everything.

They were my teachers, and now they are abandoning me. I started out as a string quartet agent with the Alban Berg and the Guarneri quartets, and my agency grew with the others who came because they were attracted by them. Almost as a matter of course, I later became the agent of the younger ones, too: of the Artemis, then the Kuss Quartet, and all the others – with the support of those who also were their teachers. I had always known that the older ones would leave at some point before I reached retirement age, but it turned out that I had no idea what it means to stay behind. I made a brief attempt to escape, with all kinds of excuses, with the idea of doing something completely different. But with the first phone call from a quartet in need, I returned to my element, discovering, happy and relieved, that this is where I belong.

Es muss sein – it must be.

BERLIN, OCTOBER 2020

I moved with my agency from Hamburg to Berlin in 2009, and Berlin is where I am writing these lines now.

Thirteen years have gone by since that 'farewell week' in Hamburg with Arnold Steinhardt and Valentin Erben. So many things have happened in this time; I could fill up another whole book – or I could just say this: they were hugely intense years, full of life.

I consider it to be a great privilege to have the opportunity to reopen the book I finished in 2007. I've been able to bring it up to date with new reflections, and, what's more, to enrich it with voices from a few of the most important string quartets of the past fifteen years.

As I have already mentioned, in 2020, the COVID-19 pandemic brought cultural life, and therefore concert life, all over the world to a complete standstill. Very many musicians have faced real hardship, as have those around them – the concert organisers and agencies.

Of course, any concert that took place during these times, against all the odds, was considered a precious gift by the artists as well as by the public. No better proof that 'the cause' lives on, and will continue to live on after COVID-19 – as it will, too, after me.

There is no end, which is why an afterword is unnecessary. Thankfulness and joy remain.

ACKNOWLEDGEMENTS

At the author's invitation, a number of her friends and clients wrote down their thoughts and experiences, exclusively for her book. Their contributions appear in italics in this edition, as do the documents made available by Günter Pichler of the Alban Berg Quartett, and also the transcript of an interview with the late leader of the LaSalle Quartet, Walter Levin.

Gregor Sigl's description of the Artemis Quartett's process of rehearsing (see pages 121–124) – as well as Sonia Simmenauer's account of her own story with the Artemis (pages 149–155) – were written in 2020 and appeared in the book's updated German edition, in February 2021. In May 2021, the Artemis Quartett announced that it was taking 'a break from performing for an indefinite period of time and [is dissolving] the current formation.'

The quotation on page 25 from Theodor W. Adorno is from *Dissonanzen: Einleitung in die Musiksoziologie* (Gesammelte Schriften, vol. 14, Suhrkamp, Frankfurt a.M. 1997, page 125). The Bernard Fournier quotations on pages 47–49 are from *L'esthétique du Quatuor à Cordes* (Fayard, Paris, 1999, pages 15–16). All translations are by us. The quotes appearing on pages 46 and 108 are from Arnold Steinhardt's book *Indivisible by Four: A String Quartet in Pursuit of Harmony* (Farrar, Straus & Giroux, New York, 1998, from pages 73 and 251 respectively). Johann Wolfgang von Goethe made his famous comment on the string quartet, mentioned on page 158, on 9 September 1828 in a letter to the composer Carl Friedrich Zelter.

We thank Wendy Körner, with whom we have spent many happy hours in and around Cambridge playing string quartets. Wendy's comments on the first draft of our translation were immensely helpful, and inspiring even where we dared to disagree. We thank Tara O'Sullivan, who accomplished her task as a copy-editor with precision, of course, but also with empathy. Thanks also to Simon Daley whose advice and art-directorial input during the final stretch of this project were invaluable, and whose patience with us was admirable.

Finally, heartfelt thanks to Sonia Simmenauer. Her combination of analytic acumen and sheer poetry is unique; her deep love for the music and for 'her' musicians is inspiring; her wisdom is enlightening. Working with her has been a real privilege.

Gwen Owen Robinson, Hartmut Kuhlmann